Praise for Ariel Gore

The End of Eve

Ariel Gore has blown my mind twice before with her previous books on motherhood and happiness – now she's stunned me a third time with *The End of Eve*. This is the story of the world's most startlingly insane, beautiful mother who was supposed to die in one year – but nearly killed her entire family and staff before she was through.

SUSIE BRIGHT, Author of *Mommy's Little Girl: Susie Bright on Sex, Motherhood, Pornography, and Cherry Pie*

Dorothy Parker famously said "there are no happy endings," but Ariel Gore's sweet, tough, elegant account of her mother's last days is absurdly happy – if happy means inhabiting life in all its mess, distress, beauty, and occasional hilarity. A near-perfect gem.

KAREN KARBO, author of *Julia Child Rules: Lessons on Savoring Life*

The depth of insight of *The End of Eve* often took my breath away. Not to mention its drop-dead humor, the sadness, and the rage. Ariel Gore's memoir is in its essence a how-to book. In the face of death, our grief, how to breathe, how to be brave, how to be funny, how to be authentic. How to make it through. But most of all: tenderness – how Ariel puts human tenderness on the page is an act of poetry damn close to sublime.

TOM SPANBAUER, author of *In The City of Shy Hunters*

Ariel Gore takes some of the heaviest life work – caring for a difficult, terminally ill parent – and somehow through her writing transforms it into a funny, interesting, moving experience. Her work is like origami in that way – capable of changing one solid thing into something entirely different, and beautiful, because of the way she looks at the world. Totally unique, and very inspiring.

CORIN TUCKER, Sleater-Kinney

How to Become a Famous Writer Before You're Dead

One of the snappiest, most useful books a writer for hire is likely to read.

DAVID PITT, *Booklist*

Hip Mama Magazine

It's the quality of the writing that sets *Hip Mama* apart.

THE NEW YORKER

Hip Mama is considered one of the best zines out there.

SAN FRANCISCO CHRONICLE

Fun and irreverent.

USA TODAY

Ariel Gore's transformation from globetrotting teenager to the hippest of mamas reads like a movie script about a Gen-X slacker following her bliss to unlikely success.

UTNE READER

Atlas of the Human Heart

Oregon Book Award finalist

Gore's adventures make absorbing reading.

BETH LEISTENSNIDER, *Booklist*

A terrific and important book. Ariel Gore rips through the cultural wasteland of the 1980s with fierce desire and female angst, taking us on a wild ride. Impossible to put down.

CORIN TUCKER, Sleater-Kinney

Bluebird: Women and the New Psychology of Happiness

Thoughtful, funny, and inspiring, Gore is a down-to-earth guide to the elusive human quest for happiness.

JUNE SAWYERS, *Booklist*

Portland Queer: Tales of the Rose City

As rough-hewn and gorgeous as the city that inspired it, this anthology breaks queer ground as it shows us that everywhere is Portland but Portland is its own special place, home to queers seeking and finding home, from the city itself to each others arms.

DAPHNE GOTTLIEB, author of *Kissing Dead Girls*

The Traveling Death and Resurrection Show

Booksense pick

This novel is a miracle – deliciously subversive and deeply spiritual.

GAYLE BRANDEIS, author of *Fruitflesh* and *The Book of Dead Birds*

An affecting tale about the search for home, connection, and authenticity.

CHRISTOPHER CASTELLANI, author of *The Saint of Lost Things*

Piercing and insightful, Gore's first novel limns one woman's complicated relationship with her religion and her personal faith.

KRISTINE HUNTLEY, Booklist

With a dash of mysticism mixed with the underground freak show scene, Ariel Gore creates a fascinating, inventive, and modern odyssey.

BETH LISICK, author of *Everybody in the Pool*

Punctuating the narrative with stories of the saints, Gore depicts Frankka's religious reawakening with both irreverence and respect for tradition and faith.

PUBLISHERS WEEKLY

A bold and imaginative story.

MICHELLE TEA, author of *Rose of No Man's Land*

Breeder: Real Life Stories from the New Generation of Mothers

Forget books that drone on about what is considered 'normal.' Scrap guides and articles that tell you how it's done...

SPIKE GILLESPIE, author of *All the Wrong Men* and *One Perfect Boy: A Memoir*

The women who gathered in my mother's kitchen when I was a child weren't free. The women whose voices are gathered in this remarkable collection are – and that's a difference worth celebrating and a development that must be documented.

DAN SAVAGE, author of *American Savage*

The Mother Trip: Hip Mama*'s Guide to Staying Sane in the Chaos of Motherhood*

Gore knows that motherhood is isolating, heartbreaking, and delightful, and she's not afraid to say so.

LINDA BECK, *Library Journal*

Ariel Gore is a brave, wise, and absolutely original voice on the subject of mothering.

HARRIET LERNER, Ph.D., author of *The Dance of Anger: A Woman's Guide to Changing the Patterns of Intimate Relationships*

Library of Congress
Cataloging-in-Publication Data

Gore, Ariel, 1970–
The End of Eve / Ariel Gore.
pages cm
ISBN 978-0-9860007-9-9
(alk. paper)

1. Parent and adult child.
2. Mothers and daughters.
3. Aging parents.
4. Mothers–Death–Psychological aspects.

I. Title.

HQ755.86.G67 2014
306.874–DC23
2013017604

Hawthorne Books
& Literary Arts

2201 Northeast 23rd Avenue
3rd Floor
Portland, Oregon 97212
hawthornebooks.com

Form:
Adam McIsaac/Sibley House

Printed in China

Set in Paperback

9 8 7 6 5 4 3 2 1

ALSO BY ARIEL GORE

Bluebird: Women and the New Psychology of Happiness
Portland Queer: Tales of the Rose City
How to Become a Famous Writer Before You're Dead
The Traveling Death and Resurrection Show
Whatever, Mom: *Hip Mama*'s Guide to Raising a Teenager
Atlas of the Human Heart
Breeder: Real Life Stories from the New Generation of Mothers
The Mother Trip: *Hip Mama*'s Guide to Staying Sane in the Chaos of Motherhood
The *Hip Mama* Survival Guide

The End of Eve

A Memoir

Ariel Gore

HAWTHORNE BOOKS & LITERARY ARTS
Portland, Oregon | MMXIV

Let everything happen to you: beauty and terror.
Just keep going. No feeling is final.

RAINER MARIA RILKE

THE END OF EVE

SOMETIMES I STILL DREAM MY MOTHER ALIVE. SHE startles me awake. Have I left a dirty dish in the sink? Written some offensive story?

In the dream, she steps out of a glass elevator into a crowded market. I'm not afraid of her, exactly. She's already seen me, anyway. So I just hover still like a hummingbird.

She points to her chest as she approaches me. Her skin is translucent like the thin skin of a water blister.

I can see her heart and lungs through that skin. I can see everything.

She squints at me. "Touch it, Ariel."

But I don't want to touch it. I know better than to touch it. If I touch it, the skin will break and it'll all come gushing out. If I touch it, I'll die soon, too. "I can't," I tell her.

She kind of scoffs at that. She says, "You were always a coward, Ariel."

But she's lying about that part.

I was a lot of things – loyal and drunk and optimistic; full of demons and stories – but I was never a coward.

All of this scared me. But I didn't run.

I'll tell you the story.

Book One

Hobo Birds

1.
All About Eve

I MUST HAVE BEEN TEN YEARS OLD WHEN MY MOTHER took me to see *Mommie Dearest* and then bragged to her friends that I'd laughed through the wire hanger scene.

She riffed on the joke at home, applying that thick white facial mask and bursting into the dark of my bedroom with the wire hanger as I slept. I'd wake terrified, her slim figure a silhouette above me, the hanger in her fist poised to come down on me. But even in interrupted half-sleep I knew my cue: I laughed. And then she wouldn't hit me.

Retelling it now it sounds so twisted, but at the time it seemed as natural as anything – fried bananas for breakfast or a flasher on the corner, all the unjudged sequences of childhood.

Where to start?

In the beginning that comes to mind, I'm grown. Thirty-nine years old. A homeowner and an unmarried wife. One kid in college and another in the crib.

Start anywhere, Ariel.

It was an ordinary day, after all. Maybe 2 p.m.

MY MOTHER STOOD on my doorstep wearing a coral sweater and coral lipstick. Her hair was white now, but she was still striking in that Hollywood kind of a way. Tiny and dark, she looked like a cross between Joan Baez and Susan Lucci from *All My Children*. Beautiful. That's the first thing people noticed about her. "Your mother is *beautiful*," they'd say. Like I didn't know.

I sat on my couch working on my laptop. I waved her inside. "That sweater looks good on you," I said.

"Thanks." She stepped over the threshold into my living room. "It was Gammie's. The sweater." She sat down in the leopard-print armchair. "This chair looks good in here."

The chair was Gammie's, too. Our dead matriarch. Our small inheritances.

I clicked the keys on my computer. My important work. I wanted to appear distracted so my mother wouldn't engage me in some conversation I didn't have time for. I had to finish a blog for *Psychology Today*. I had to post a few story critiques in the online class I was teaching. I had to pick my son up from preschool in an hour. My mother was just stopping by to get the youthful skin serum made from sake and lamb placenta that she'd ordered on the internet, wasn't she? What did she need to talk about?

She cleared her throat. "I guess I should tell you. I didn't get what I wanted."

I glanced up at her. I knew she wanted an exposed-brick condo downtown. I shrugged. "There'll be another condo." Portland was sprouting new condos like goat grass.

My mother didn't say anything.

I felt something like a chill in my hand. I hadn't had a cigarette in three years, but now I wanted one. I stopped typing, looked up at her.

Sitting there in my Gammie's old chair, my mother seemed so small. She didn't smile or frown. "It's cancer," she said.

"What?" It was like I'd heard the syllables, but didn't know their meaning.

"It's lung cancer." Her words floated into the air between us like dandelion seeds, just hung there.

"What?"

I'd seen the scans at the hospital two weeks earlier, the little Christmas lights that filled my mother's rib cage. The pulmonologist wore red shoes. He pointed to those Christmas lights, said he was worried. But she'd never been a smoker. There were still so many different things it could be.

"I have lung cancer," my mother said again.

I moved the computer from my lap, sat up straight. "Shit. All right. What do we do?"

"Nothing." She fiddled with the gold band on her ring finger. "It's too late for chemo."

I remembered summer mornings when I was a kid, sneaking away from the violence of our home to make daisy chains in the park down the street; I remembered that just then for no reason.

"What do you mean we do nothing?"

"Stage four," she said. "I'll be dead in a year." She reached into her purse, grabbed her coral lipstick, and re-applied. She licked her teeth. "I'll go home now," she said. Home to the studio apartment I'd just rented for her next to the pawn shop on 82nd Avenue.

"Oh, stay for dinner," I tried.

"No." My mother pushed herself up out of my grandmother's chair. "I don't want to drive back in the dark."

MY MOTHER HAD finally rented a car after all three major cab companies in Portland banned her. I couldn't even get a taxi to the airport these days when I called from my landline. They associated my number with her. "Eve," the operators would insist. "We know it's you."

"They have ego problems" is all she'd say about the cab drivers and the dispatchers when I asked how she'd managed to offend them. "Unbelievable ego problems."

"Listen," I said. "I have to go pick up Maxito. Sol should be home by six. We'll bring dinner to your place?"

My mother nodded. "All right. But it's got to be organic."

"Of course."

She stood up, moved for the door, then turned back to me.

"Don't tell your sister about this," she said. "She's channeling Pele on the Big Island. We don't want to ruin her retreat."

"Okay," I agreed.

And my mother was gone.

PELE? MAYBE I should have been channeling Pele.

Instead my girlfriend, Sol, and I had been taking care of my mother for three years. She'd come to Portland for a hip replacement, second hip replacement, minor stroke and too-long recovery. It all started after my stepdad died. The California newspapers called his death in Mexico a suicide: *Local Excommunicated Catholic Priest Takes Own Life*. It was almost as good as the headlines of my childhood: *Local Priest Defrocked by Temptress Named Eve*. But it wasn't suicide. Not exactly. Either my mother killed him or they were in on it together. He wasn't young. Eighty nine to my mother's sixty four. Maybe he was sick. My mother had always talked about "mercy killing" when people had terminal illnesses. But in his last email, my stepdad said "God bless Dr. Kevorkian."

Precisely how it ended is one of the things we don't get to know.

"You can't ever know what happens between people," my first journalism teacher used to say. Her words stunned me even though I knew she was right.

She was incredibly sexy, that professor, with her square-rimmed glasses. And I had a problem with transference. I hung on her sultry morning words and here she was dashing all hope for certainty.

Never mind that the idea that truth was discoverable had been one of the things that drew me to journalism – over, say, poetry or women's studies.

You can't ever know what happens between people. That's what she said. So, there I had it.

Either my mom killed my stepdad or they were in on it together and who cares anyway because here now my mother was sick and she was going to need someone to take care of her. And here we were. Too late for chemo.

I'D NEVER GIVEN much brain-space to the idea that my mother would die in her 60s or even her 70s. My Gammie had just died a month earlier at 91.

Does death always arrive first as an idea?

My first big death was a childhood friend. She'd had cancer for a few years, done it all: amputation and remission, chemo and visualization, macrobiotics and metastasis. It hadn't been too late for anything. Surely my friend would survive. She called me a few days before she died to warn me. "I'm trying to stay focused on a picture of me healthy at the beach in Hawaii, but sometimes I just get an image of myself cold and gray in my coffin."

An image is an idea.

We were twelve years old.

THAT EVENING IN Portland after I got the idea that my mother would die didn't feel very different from any other evening in Portland. It was raining.

I picked Maxito up from preschool and he recounted his day to me in his toddler-Spanglish and "*no me gusta* take a tubby."

When Sol came home and let the door slam behind her I jumped, just a little, not sure if she was angry about something at work or if I'd left the porch muddy.

My mother called and said never mind dinner, she wanted to watch a Bette Davis movie alone.

Sol and Maxito and I ate rice and black beans at our little round kitchen table and Maxito flung the beans at the wall and said "too *spicy*," but he ate a few spoonsful of rice before he climbed out of his chair and toddled away from the table.

Sol rolled a joint. Sol. She was strong and pretty with sparkling eyes that seemed almost magic until she'd confessed that those golden flecks were actually citric acid burns because someone back in the Dominican Republic when she was a kid told her that lime juice would turn her brown eyes blue. I still thought her eyes were magical, but now they reminded me of the meanness in people, too.

Who would tell that to a child?

She lit her joint, offered it to me like she always did and I refused it like I always did. The olive skin of her arm was half-covered in tattoos of spiders and saints.

I knocked back a beer. A couple of beers.

AS I NURSED Maxito in the moonlit dark of our bedroom that night, I whispered to Sol, "What are we going to do?"

She sighed the way you sigh when bad things feel inevitable. "I read the Merck manual online at work today," she said. She ran a sliding-scale community veterinary clinic between our house and the bar I frequented. "Your mom isn't going to live a year. She has maybe two months if she doesn't treat it. Six months maximum. Stage four lung cancer is no joke."

I stared at the giant painting on our bedroom wall. Three hobo birds gathered around a pot of stew over a campfire.

Maxito had fallen asleep nursing. He released my nipple from his mouth-grip as his breath changed. I waited a few moments to be sure he wouldn't wake, then carried him to the crib in the little room that used to be my office.

"Ariel?" Sol whispered when I crawled back under the flowered quilt.

"Uh huh?"

"I don't think I have the mortgage money this month."

"Hmmm."

Sol turned over, curled her back to me as she fell asleep.

My hobo birds in the moonlight.

WHEN SOL STARTED to snore, I tiptoed out into the kitchen, poured myself a little mason jar of whiskey, lit a seven-day candle on my altar. I settled onto the red couch in the living room, pretended the glow from my laptop screen had a warmth to it–like some woodstove in some little cabin.

I knew I had to call my daughter, Maia, in Los Angeles. I knew I had to call my sister, Leslie, even if my mother didn't want me to. But they could both wait until morning. I clicked to Facebook, saw my old friend Teagan online. Maybe Teagan could find the pony in all this.

ME:

What am I going to do? Sol isn't like a partner, she's the roommate from hell who doesn't even pay the rent. And now my mom is dying.

TEAGAN:

Are we allowed to joke about lesbian bed death?

ME:

No. And don't try to tell me it doesn't happen to straight people. When they stop having sex they just call it "marriage."

TEAGAN:

LOL. First you get U-Hauled and now this. What's up with your mom?

ME:

Stage IV lung cancer. They told her she has a year.

TEAGAN:

I'm sorry to hear that. But, you now, if it's any comfort, your mom won't be dead in a year.

ME:

How do you figure?

TEAGAN:

I've met your mom. She's a narcissist. Narcissists take a long time to die.

ME:

You're funny.

TEAGAN:
I'm serious.

ME:
What do I do?

TEAGAN:
Do you remember when we were in our early 20s and I got pregnant and you already had Maia? Do you remember your advice?

ME:
No.

TEAGAN:
You told me not to think on it too hard. You said everything is freedom and everything is loneliness. You said there's no regret and there's no sacrifice. You said make your choice and let the rest fall away.

ME:
That's your advice to me now?

TEAGAN:
Yep. Everything is freedom and everything is loneliness. Make your choice and let the rest fall away.

ME:
Maybe I should get that tattooed on my wrist.

TEAGAN:
You should. You haven't posted a new tattoo on Facebook in months. Anyway, look, I'm tired and overmedicated. Talk to you soon?

SHE FLICKERED OFFLINE before I could answer. I poured myself another jar of whiskey, took a too-big sip and held it in my throat to savor the sting and heat of it. Even with my glasses on, the walls of my living room started to recede into that familiar blur. I must have fallen asleep, but I didn't dream.

AT DAWN I crawled back into bed next to Sol, drifted in and out as I listened to her breath. Visions of my mother getting sicker floated across my dreamspace. Visions of my mother in a hospital bed in the little room that used to be my office. Visions of my mother getting thinner.

How am I going to take care of her?

For three years of doctors' appointments and physical therapists and assisted care facilities, the light at the end of the tunnel had always been that she was going to get better and go home to her house in southern Mexico and get old like a normal person.

Now maybe the only light was death.

My house felt too small for all of us.

The sound of morning rain.

Anywhere else in the world I loved that sound – cleansing and life-giving – but in Portland that incessant noise was just irritating. Like needles hitting tin.

How am I going to take care of her?

Sol woke mumbling "Oh, Bipa..."

Bipa. The master mime from the circus Sol had performed with when she was in her 20s. It still bothered me when Sol woke with that name on her lips. I'd found a half-dozen love notes to that woman over the years. They'd flutter out from between Neruda pages: *Dearest Bipa, Beautiful and Silent Bipa, My Soul Mate Bipa* ... You'd think I'd have gotten used to it by now, gotten used to Bipa, but Sol's whispered longings still made me feel nauseous and jaded. Still inspired me to put my boots on and walk the two blocks to the Twilight Room, to slip into a vinyl booth and order a double shot of Big Bottom with a beer back. But it was too early for whiskey now.

I crept into Maxito's room, watched him in his crib as he slept, watched the rise and fall of his chest.

I missed Maia living at home. Some mornings even when she was a teenager I'd poke my head into her basement room, listen for the sound of her breath to tell me she was still alive.

Watching Maxito now, I felt that sudden sadness when you know you can only promise your children suffering. I tried to shake it off. Maia was doing fine in college in Los Angeles. Maxito seemed happy enough. Who was I to project my existential depression onto them? Every day we were still breathing somehow, even when breath seemed like such a fragile thing.

Pull yourself together, Ariel.

In the kitchen, I set the yellow kettle on the flame to boil. "Oh, Bipa." I said it under my breath and all overdramatic like I could make it sound too stupid to matter. "I love you, Bipa." *I mean, seriously? A mime?*

Maybe all I needed was some strong black coffee.

2.
Pele, Have Mercy

"DUDE, IT'S THE CRACK OF DAWN HERE." MY SISTER'S sleepy voice on the phone gave me a sudden unexpected hope. Like rose petals in the rain. Like maybe this wasn't going to be so bad after all. It was just cancer. Families handled this kind of thing all the time. The two of us would think of something. Maybe we'd even bond over it.

"Sorry," I said. "I forgot the time difference." I sat on the front steps of my house, watching the overcast autumn morning. Two months earlier I would have called my Gammie for advice. Two years earlier I would have called my stepdad. Death was relentless, but I still had my sister.

If we're mostly water, DNA, and memory, then a sister is something. We shared the same blood – the same biological parents, anyway. We'd grown up in the same old house with the same mother and the same stepdad and the same brown rice and apple juice potluck dinners. We'd stood side by side against the same wall when we were in trouble for a B on a report card or a stain on a flowered rug; we'd waited there for our mother to bash our heads together or into the plaster wall.

Yes, if anyone could understand the exact nature of my ambivalence, it would be my sister.

"How's the retreat going?"

"It's all right," Leslie sighed. "I'm in this little hotel near the volcano. Palm trees. What's up?"

I felt like a jerk calling my sister before my mother wanted me to, but it seemed weird to keep the secret. "It's bad," I started. I took a breath and counted to three, but when I finally blurted it all, about the lung cancer and the year to live, Leslie didn't seem surprised.

"That explains the dead birds in my dreams," she said.

I heard the flick of her lighter and all at once remembered my loneliness. My sister's ambivalence had always been a different color than mine.

"I totally dreamed this," she said. I could hear her sucking on her cigarette. "Anyway, don't worry about it."

An androgynous Portland hipster biked past my house, balanced a huge cup of coffee between a free hand and the handlebars.

"I *am* worried," I squeaked. "I'm the one who has to take care of her."

Leslie cigarette-exhaled into the phone. "You don't *have* to do anything. Anyway Mom won't get sick. She'll take herself out."

A few cars passed. Fat raindrops started to fall. One of my cats purred against my leg.

"Listen," my sister said. "I've been doing this spiritual work here on the Big Island and I've been in contact with one of our unknown ancestors. It's a Cherokee woman who was raped and murdered and beheaded. I'm just now realizing that this woman is the reason we don't trust men. She's the reason there are hardly any men in our family."

I nodded like my sister could see me. I didn't think of myself as someone who didn't trust men, but I wasn't going to argue. "That sounds about right," I mumbled.

Maxito tapped on the window behind me, giggled as he pressed his nose against the glass and made it fog with his breath.

The sight of him made my tits swell with milk.

"Well anyway, listen," I said. "Maxito's up. I gotta go. Talk to you soon?"

I heard my sister's lighter flick again. "I'm flying home in a couple of days," she said. "Talk then?"

I clicked the phone off, tapped the windowpane in front of Maxito's face. "Morning, baby."

I craved salted chocolate, craved so many things right then, but settled for nursing my toddler on our soft red couch. I could hear Sol in the kitchen steaming coconut milk for my second cup of coffee and I felt like such a brat. I wondered if this was a pattern for me – this always craving something I didn't have. People's mothers got cancer all the time. People without sisters or money or health insurance or sex lives or salted chocolate. They didn't whine about it. Women all over the world were caregivers even if they were breadwinners, too. They dealt with it.

I balanced Maxito on my knee as I nursed him, reached for the Sharpie pen on the coffee table in front of me, wrote on the inside of my wrist: *Behave in a way you're going to be proud of.* I didn't know what I meant by that, exactly, didn't know what I'd be proud of, if anything. But the words seemed important.

Sol set my coffee in front of me.

"Thanks, honey," I said. And I meant it – wanted to mean it – wanted to appreciate Sol even if all she could do was make me a cup of coffee with steamed coconut milk. "Can you take Maxito to preschool? I have to pick my mom up for an oncology appointment."

"Sure," Sol smiled sad. "Whatever you need."

3. Agendas

MY MOTHER FIGURED THE ONCOLOGIST WOULD BE French. "With a name like that he's got to be French," she said as she climbed into the passenger seat of my little Honda.

Maybe she was thinking he'd be handsome, too – elegant and refined. Maybe they'd have an affair. He'd be open to treating the cancer with an organic diet or with magnesium-rich Epsom salts. He was European, after all. "Europeans are always much more open to alternative therapies," my mother said.

I turned north on 82nd, stopped at the light. "What should we ask him? What's our agenda?"

My mother stared ahead into the rain. I knew her well enough to know that she always had an agenda, but sometimes part of her agenda was pretending she didn't have an agenda. "We just let him talk," she said. "He'll have an agenda."

"Should we ask, you know, I mean, if you do get sick, should we ask him if your insurance covers long-term care or, you know, home care?"

My mother coughed. "That's depressing. That makes me cough."

THERE WERE NO windows in the oncology waiting room.

"I'm here to see Doctor *Benwaaa*." My mother dragged out the end of the name and silenced the *t*.

The receptionist tapped her keyboard. "Ya mean Doctor Bin-oyt?"

My mother frowned. "Isn't he French?"

The receptionist shrugged. "Doubt it."

Fill out these forms.

Weigh in behind door number one.

Blood pressure behind door number two.

Wait behind door number three.

OF COURSE DOCTOR Benoit wasn't French. Doctor Benoit wasn't a he, either.

In walks a sixty-something woman with long, stringy hair and not a stitch of makeup. She looked like the Catholic Worker types my stepdad used to hang out with. Beige plaid pants. Wrinkled white coat over a beige shirt. She sat down on a chair with little wheels on it, scooted in too close to us. I thought to tell her to please move back, that I didn't know where she was from, but here on the West Coast of the United States we allowed for a certain amount of personal space. I glanced at my mother, but she didn't seem uncomfortable, so I kept quiet. Doctor Benoit could sit close if she wanted to.

The last doctor, the pulmonologist, the one with the red shoes, paged through my mother's chart and showed us scans on computer screens. But this doctor had no paperwork, no images. She just sat in front of us, sat too close. It occurred to me that I might be dreaming all this. I thought, *I'll scream and if a sound comes out I'll know this is happening*. But I didn't open my mouth.

"The kind of cancer you have is called adenocarcinoma," the oncologist said. She looked at my mom, then at me. "It's the most common type of lung cancer."

She asked my mother questions.

Yes and no.

More questions.

"I smoked one cigarette a day for about a year when I was twenty," my mother said.

"I never lived with anyone who smoked," my mother said.

"I have a cough, but it's nothing," my mother said.

"It's because I moved into a new apartment and I didn't have a comforter for the first few nights," my mother said.

"I was cold, so I got a cough," my mother said.

"I've lost a little weight," my mother said, "but it's just because I started this vegan diet and I don't know what I can eat. I haven't found enough I can eat."

"I'm not as active as I used to be," my mother said, "but it's because of the new hip."

"I feel fine," my mother said.

The oncologist nodded. She didn't seem to have an agenda. "Do you have any questions for me?"

My mother held her hand out to inspect her manicure, didn't look up. "Yes," she said. "How long will I live?"

I looked at the little sink next to me and the white cupboards above, the exam table in the corner behind the chair on wheels.

"Well," the oncologist finally said. "That's the hardest question. This does seem to be a slow-growing cancer. I suspect you've had it for a couple of years."

A COUPLE OF years. I thought about that. It had been a couple of years since my stepdad died. Since my mother killed him or they were in on it together. I glanced at my wrist: *Behave in a way that you're going to be proud of.*

Now would not be a good time to scream.

"It isn't smoking-related," the oncologist was saying. "You're female. Both these things improve your prognosis. I don't know how long you'll live." She looked up at the clock, like maybe my mother only had a matter of hours. "I would guess a year," her tone stayed flat, like she was telling us a stranger's address. "A year would be my guess." The oncologist looked at me now. "Do you have any questions, Ariel?"

Of course I had questions. A year, but what would the year look like? Would my mother be all right for a while – three or six months – and then collapse? Would she continue on this slow energy decline we'd all been forced to endure with her – the decline that had her moving in and out of assisted living facilities where Sol and I took turns bringing organic breakfasts and Ayurvedic dinners until my mother had the inevitable late-night panic attack and decided the room was bugged and the nurses were Eastern-bloc spies and her neighbors were trying to poison her and we'd finally relent and find her someplace new? Would it be like *Terms of Endearment*? Would we have to buy a bigger house so she could come and live with us? Would it be like *Grey Gardens*? Would we all start drinking vodka for breakfast? Would it be like *Whatever Happened to Baby Jane*?

My mother coughed. "No," she answered for me. "Ariel doesn't have any questions."

I didn't say anything, didn't want to make my mother cough with my questions, so I just stood up and my mother stood up and Dr. Benoit stood up and we all shook hands like we'd just made some terrible business deal.

IN THE ELEVATOR, my mother coughed. "Ariel," she said, "I just want you to know that if I do get sick, you won't have to take care of me."

"I don't mind," I told her. "I can take care of you. Or we can hire someone. Or both, you know – whatever you feel comfortable with."

I remembered what my friend China wrote in her punk parenting zine when we were young moms. "I want to be the female Bukowski, the female Burroughs, but instead I'm just the female." In that elevator right then, I felt like such the female – the caregiver.

My mother shook her head, looked down at her gray Ugg boots. "If I ever need a caretaker, I'll just blow my brains out."

"Well," I laughed. "On that cheery note."

My mother laughed, too, but then she sucked in her cheeks. "I'm serious," she said.

WE INCHED BACK through the traffic to my mother's apartment. NPR was having a pledge drive. I stopped in the parking lot, but my mother didn't make a move to get out of the car. I wondered if she wanted me to come around and open the door for her – if she wanted me to walk her inside her building. Maybe I was supposed to treat her differently now that we knew she would die soon. I glanced at my wrist. "I have to go pick up Maxito," I said.

"I know." She nodded. "It's just. Announcement."

I wasn't sure I could handle another announcement, but I took a good breath. "Yes?"

"I won't die on 82nd," she said "I *refuse* to die on 82nd Avenue."

82nd Avenue. Most of the prostitutes had been gentrified further east by now, but the street was still mostly fast food chains and bus stops. "All right," I said. Fair enough. The apartment on 82nd was only meant to be temporary, anyway. Until she got better and packed up and headed home to southern Mexico, to her art studio and her friends there.

I couldn't picture her dying in that tiny apartment, either, but where could she die? She'd already been through half the hotels and adult foster care homes in Portland, through house-sits and retirement complexes where they played Bingo on Thursday nights and served the white bread roast beef sandwiches she was too good to eat.

"Where do you want to ... live?"

WHEN I WAS a kid my mom always offered our guest room to our aging relatives – to my great-grandmother and then to Gammie. "Your room is ready," she told them when their husbands died or when they hit 72 or 84.

They refused her offers, of course. "Oh, darling," they said, "I don't want to be a burden."

"How could they refuse?" my mother cried over our brown rice dinner. "This is the Mexican way – the generations living together."

I thought it was a weird thing to say. I mean, we weren't Mexican. In all other circumstances my mother claimed Italian roots in southern Texas, but somehow when it came to elder-care she needed to be Mexican.

NOW SHE STARED at me. "We can just get a big house –" she started.

I should have said no right then.

I didn't owe her anything.

"I can't die on 82nd," she pleaded.

Her words made my heart feel small in my chest, but logic still said no.

"Think about it, Tiniest?"

She still called me by my childhood nickname, the one she coined I guess because I was the baby in the family. "Of course." I started to put my hand on her shoulder, but she moved away from me. "We'll figure something out," I promised.

"Okay," she said softly.

And I watched as my mother walked away from my car in the rain, one of her legs dragging a little.

NPR still hadn't met their pledge goal for the break. I texted Sol: *My mom wants us all to get a big house together.*

Sol texted right back: *No way.*

But that night after we put Maxito to bed and I opened a second bottle of five-dollar red wine and Sol picked the dregs of her weed from her little wooden stash box and we listened to Lucinda Williams, she nodded to the music and said, "Okay."

She filled her rolling paper with bits of weed. "We're going to have to take care of your mom wherever she lives, right?"

I shrugged. "Probably." The Virgin of Guadalupe tattoo on Sol's forearm was already getting that weathered look. She'd gotten it when her own mom died a few years earlier. Her mother had been ill for at least a decade, but she was far away in the Dominican Republic so we never took care of her, never had to.

Sol rolled her little joint. "And there's pretty much no chance your mom's going to live even a year."

"According to your Merck Manual, anyway."

"Right? We can do anything for a year." Sol licked her rolling paper. "So what if we get a place with her? Just not in Portland?"

I thought Portland had been good to Sol – she had good friends and a thriving veterinary practice even if she refused to charge more than fifteen dollars to set a dog's broken bone or to put a cat down – but Sol had always hated Portland. Too much rain, too many white people. We'd been here nine years, but it wasn't my home either. We were what lots of people were in Portland – displaced from where we'd come from because we were overly tattooed or queer or couldn't afford the rent where we were born. We'd come to Portland because it didn't matter. The real estate was cheap, and people read all kinds of books here.

Sol stood up and turned the stove on, lit her joint from the burner.

I knew where Sol wanted to go.

She'd lived outside Santa Fe in her 20s, always romanticized that high desert. "If I'm ever going to make a living," she said, "it's going to be in New Mexico."

I tried to imagine that, Sol finally making a living.

"If I'm ever really going to be a musician," she said, "it's going to be in New Mexico." She swayed to the music now. "I've done your thing here in Portland all these years. But you can be a writer anywhere." She looked past me, like she could already see her new life. "Honestly, if you and I are ever going to have a sex life, it's going to be in New Mexico." She exhaled a plume of smoke toward me. "That place is the salve to my soul."

New Mexico. It sounded crazy, but maybe it wasn't crazier than anything else. Maybe this was my chance to make everyone happy. My mother would get us, Sol would get New Mexico, and I'd get – well – maybe Sol was right that I could live anywhere. At least I'd get out of the rain.

Sol kissed me on the head. I always felt like a little kid when she did that, not like anybody's girlfriend. "Think about it," she said.

But all I could think about right then was my mother placing some pawn-shop gun in her mouth and pulling the trigger.

4. I ♥ My Garden

I'D ALMOST ALWAYS SLEPT THROUGH THE PREDAWN train that shook my little house as it rumbled through the railyard, but now I opened my eyes in the dark morning and my mind started typing 400 words a minute: *Where am I going to get a hospital bed? Will it fit in Maxito's room? Then maybe Maxito can sleep in here with Sol and me? Should I call my aunt Laurie? She's a medical reporter. She might know things. Should I stop eating dairy products? Did I imagine that having a baby would save my relationship with Sol? How cliché is that? Why hasn't my mother's biopsy wound healed? Would it be wrong to find a lover on Craigslist? Would it be safe? What if I answered an anonymous ad and it was someone I already knew? One of my students or one of Sol's clients? What if I recognized their pet goat? What's the difference between a heavy drinker and an alcoholic? I need to do a money magnetism spell to manifest the mortgage. Do most words start with M? My mother has lost weight, hasn't she? What if we don't have as long as the doctors say? I need to lose weight. I can't get a lover on Craigslist until I lose weight. Is the fact that I can't fathom a miracle cancer cure a form of negative thinking? Does negative thinking kill people? Why does my brain still seem to use a typewriter? Will my kids think in Facebook updates long after the death of Facebook?*

I didn't hear rain, but couldn't believe there wasn't any. Maybe I'd become desensitized to that irritating sound. Either way, I needed out of my house, out of my brain. I put on a hoodie and boots over my sleeping sweats, ducked out the backdoor and ambled through the rainless mist toward the all-night gas station where there was always a giant cup of weak coffee with chalky creamer waiting for me.

"You so sexy even in the morning," the guy at the register said as he ran my card. He was clean-shaven and unappealing.

I rolled my eyes. "Thanks, I guess?"

"Just a simple compliment," he yelled as the glass door shut behind me. I sipped the hot coffee. There was always something satisfying about a terrible cup of coffee too early in Portland.

I crossed the street, climbed through a hole in the chain-link fence that held the train tracks, and I crouched there in the weeds and the garbage.

I remembered an afternoon a few years before my Gammie died. We were poolside under a California sky. She placed her hand over her heart the way she did when she was thinking life-thoughts. "I may look old," she said. She was in her late 80s. "But your core never changes. Inside, I could be eighteen years old."

I felt like a teenager now, bent against the morning.

The graffiti that covered the wall on the far side of the train tracks was so impossibly bright, I thought of Van Gogh. Maybe I was slipping into some artistic depression that caused me to envision the world more vivid than it actually was.

I don't want to lose an ear over all this.

Another train.

My brain.

When my mother was pregnant with me, she knew I'd be a boy. She was so excited. Imagine that. A boy. In our family? She'd name me Claiborne after our great-great-grand-uncle, the first governor of Louisiana. "Napoleon sold, Jefferson bought, Claiborne signed," my great grandma Addie used to brag. *Governor Claiborne*. He once danced with Marie Laveau herself. "People called those voodooiennes evil," Addie said. "But those women just knew how to make things happen. They were the problem solvers."

When I showed up all shiny-wet and obviously female, my

mother just looked at me. It wasn't even 6 p.m. according to my birth certificate – midsummer in a California hospital – but my mother claims the sky outside was indigo night.

A nurse took me away and my mother fell asleep, woke alone in darkness and didn't bother to name me. Another girl.

I sipped my gas station coffee as a freight train barreled past.

Your core stays the same.

ONCE I WAS four and my mother told me a story. She was actually a witch who flew around at night in a mortar and she'd kidnapped me from my real parents. At first I laughed at her story, but she was serious. "Don't you see this mole on my nose, Tiniest?" she pointed with her red-manicured nail. "It proves I'm a witch. Do any of the other mommies at Lad and Lass Preschool have moles on their noses?" She kind of cackled.

The next day and the next day I watched as the other women brought their uncombed children to Lad and Lass Preschool. My mother was right. No moles. I was some kind of an orphan. Stolen. I wondered if my real parents were looking for me.

ONCE I WAS nine, morning paper route finished and the street lights still on. A Southern Pacific hurdled past. I loved those trains. I pedaled as fast as I could, just trying to keep up. In my good childhood memories I'm always in motion. And there are never any parents.

ONCE I WAS sixteen, running rushing flying away from home. Ten thousand miles was never far enough. I scrawled *Escape Artist* on the soles of my feet with a Sharpie pen, got my first tattoo – a bird on my back.

Everything was freedom and everything was loneliness.

Another train.

My gas station coffee getting cold.

And I wasn't a kid anymore.

IN THE GRAY light of dawn, I crept back into my little house. Sol and Maxito were still asleep, but my cellphone on the kitchen counter already buzzed with messages from my mother's friends and mine.

Everyone who called in those early days after my mother's diagnosis had big ideas. They knew someone who knew someone who'd cured themselves of late-stage cancer with herbal tea or mass quantities of blueberries. They had a naturopath who specialized in figuring out which shampoos a person was allergic to. They knew someone who had a lead on a maligned American doctor who now practiced exclusively in Mexico. They had the address of a shaman in Cleveland, a meditation teacher in Manhattan. They remembered a woman they'd met at a party who'd mentioned a book – they'd find out the title. They knew a website where we could order a little-known healing mushroom from a curandera in the forest in Idaho.

I distracted myself with academic articles on death. In "Dying in a Technological Society," the brainy doctor Eric Cassell claimed that our attitudes about death boiled down to cultural mythologies. Americans had moved from a moral mythology to a technological mythology, so we'd come to see death as something that could be overcome. Death was like a broken appliance – just a mechanical problem to be investigated, solved, and fixed.

My mother intended to solve this death problem. Instead of sleep, she sat at her computer researching the latest alternative therapies and buying tinctures, vitamins, size-six Mephisto boots, and antique French dishes.

Every afternoon, the UPS guy piled my front porch with boxes of things that had no resale value.

My mother had just inherited $100,000 from my Gammie. It was her prerogative, I kept telling myself, if she wanted to spend it all online in three weeks. But I was worried, too. What if we needed more than my mother's monthly social security check to take care of her?

The phone kept ringing.

I DIDN'T KNOW why we were going to see oncologist #2.

My mother didn't want any Western treatments, but she still seemed to want something from these doctors. Maybe just some acknowledgment that she was right.

I read *On Death and Dying*. According to Elisabeth Kübler-Ross, the first emotional stage after a terminal diagnosis is denial. But my mother had moved straight into anger.

"Oh, just go with her to the second oncologist," Maia said on the phone when I finally talked to her.

And I would. Of course I would.

"I want to come home," Maia said. "I want to spend some time with Nonna."

My daughter was maybe the only one in the family who loved my mother without reservation – and it wasn't because she hadn't seen the brutal part. Maia just didn't expect people to come without shadows any more than she expected the sky to come without clouds. She'd seen too much death for a 19-year-old, and she understood that life didn't come without cancer.

"There's time," I promised her. "Do your schoolwork, come home at break." The semester would be over in five or six weeks. "Give my love to the boyfriend," I said.

"Okay," Maia sighed. "Promise to call me if anything gets worse?"

"I promise."

She hadn't had time to get to the hospital in London when we got word that her father was dying.

"I seriously promise."

IN THE ONCOLOGY waiting room without any windows, the receptionist was having a hot flash. I held Maxito on my hip, rocked him back and forth as the receptionist fanned herself with a hospice brochure. Her acrylic nails were airbrushed with palm trees. "This is a nightmare," she said. "How do I make them stop?"

"Chinese herbs," my mother told her, and she dug around

in her purse for her herbalist's business card. "You just have to drink a tea from hell every morning."

The receptionist kept fanning herself. "I can do that." She typed something into the computer as she talked, her nails click-clacking on the keys. She squinted at my mother's medical card. "This is a *living* nightmare," she sighed.

"I'll trade places with you," my mother offered.

The receptionist didn't say anything. She nodded at the computer screen. "I'll think about that."

"Yeah," my mother said. "Think about it real hard. And get yourself some herbs."

MY MOTHER TOOK off her Uggs to weigh in. One hundred eleven pounds. "Pretty good," she said to the nurse. "Right? A cancer patient only losing a couple of pounds?"

The nurse shrugged. "You'll lose weight when you start chemo."

Maxito wiggled in my arms. He didn't like the fluorescent lights as the nurse escorted us all into the same little white room where we'd met oncologist #1.

I set up Maxito's DVD player on the exam table, pressed play.

"Snoopy doops?" Maxito smiled. "I like Linus."

My mother smiled in his direction, but she was busy shuffling papers, gearing up for a fight. "Chemo," she hummed. "As if I would take their Chemo. Is it totally foreign to all these Western medical practitioners that I might not want to poison myself?"

And here comes oncologist #2, a guy with a slouch and an *I ♥ My Garden* T-shirt.

He sat down on the chair with wheels and smiled at us. "I understand you want to learn about Tarceva."

"I've actually read quite a bit online," my mother started. Her hands, in particular, seemed very small. "I hear they call it the chemo pill."

Oncologist #2 sort of nodded.

"I understand it has quite a few side effects, including terrible rashes and will only prolong my life by a matter of a couple of months?"

Oncologist #2 nodded again, didn't say anything.

Maxito bounced and bobbed to the Snoopy song.

"Do you garden?" My mother smiled at oncologist #2, but her voice had that tone.

I wanted to disappear.

"Yes I do," the oncologist perked up. "I garden."

"Organic?" My mother scooted her reading glasses down her nose to get a better look at the guy.

"Yes. Organic." He smiled, like now we were talking about something interesting.

"Well," my mother seethed. "Would you put Tarceva on your precious fucking organic garden?"

Oncologist #2 just kind of stared at my mother, then glanced at me, at Maxito riveted to his Peanuts video.

My mom narrowed her gaze, wanting to argue with the doctor.

But oncologist #2 was aloof. "No," he said. "I wouldn't put Tarceva in my garden. Your research is accurate."

As we left, my mother leaned into me and whispered, "That guy had NO ego. Drop me off at the Anthropologie downtown, will you?"

I DIDN'T WANT to go straight home either, so after we dropped her at the store, I headed for the Sapphire Hotel on Hawthorne Boulevard where everything was red and haunted by the ghosts of dead sailors and whores. Maxito could entertain himself with a cheese platter in that place long enough for me to nurse a happy hour "Seven Sins" and run into somebody who'd remind me why I loved this rainy city.

But no one I knew was at the Sapphire Hotel that night.

"Can I get you anything else, ma'am?" The bar waitress had tattoos of bacon and cupcakes on her chest.

I'd been in Portland for ten years and it occurred to me that I'd suddenly become older than almost everyone else and now I had this toddler at the bar and who was I to think I belonged anywhere?

When I first bought my house by the railyard, I held onto the doorframes sometimes and looked at the sills under the leaded windows and thought, I own this, even though the bank mostly owned it. Now as Maxito played with his cheese and laughed, I felt my ribs through my hoodie, uneven, and I thought, *this is what I own*, bones and flesh – this is my structure.

AT HOME THAT night I took a random book from the shelf.

The Upanishads.

I ran my hand across the gold cover, asked: *Should I or should I not agree to live with my mother ... move my family and my life ... change everything?*

I opened to a random page and read this: "Live with me for a year. Then you may ask questions."

So there it was.

You make your choice and let the rest fall away.

I DIDN'T WANT to answer the phone, but Vivian's name flashed and Vivian was half a Buddhist and she loved me beyond reason. Surely Vivian could understand when I explained my plan and that maybe this was my dharma – my spiritual work right now. But Vivian just clucked her tongue when I said that. "It's not your dharma, honey," she snapped. "It's your Co-DA."

As I hung up, I wondered at the difference.

Seemed like maybe dharma work was the compassionate service you offered because you were on a spiritual path, here to let everything happen to you, to expose yourself to annihilation in hopes of burning through to some indestructible core of tenderness and confidence.

And then Co-DA was the compassionate service you offered because you were a total and complete sucker.

5. Mother as Metaphor

I WAS IN A CAFÉ ON HAWTHORNE GRABBING A CUP OF coffee after my morning teaching gig when my phone rang.

Maia. "Hey, Mama, I'm driving home for winter break."

I stared at a painting on the wall. A black bird on a wire, a hazy red sky behind it. A Portland painting. "Don't drive, Honey. Just fly. You have a free ticket on Southwest." It was fifteen hours on the I-5 from Los Angeles to Portland. All those snowy passes.

"I want to drive, Mama. I want to have my car when I'm home."

Her plan was ridiculous, of course, but what difference would it make at this point? I was trying not to ask too many questions. *That's what the oracle advised, right?* No questions for a year, anyway. I'd take my hands off the controls of this life thing and see what happened.

IT HAD BEEN six weeks since my mother's diagnosis. She'd lost weight, but she still drove around town in her bright blue rental car in the rain and somehow found the energy to yell at service workers.

She'd jumped at the idea of moving to Santa Fe. "Perfect. All the artists live there, don't they?"

So I was getting my little house ready to put on the market. "Beiging it up," my friend at the paint store said when I came in for ever more cans of light brown and pale yellow to cover the oranges and blues.

"You never can be too beige in this market."

Between my mom's inheritance and the expected money from the sale of my place, we'd come up with enough to make an offer on a for-sale-by-owner stucco duplex on an acre of land on a dirt road in Santa Fe. We'd given up visiting oncologists and settled on a fairly simple treatment plan for my mother: weekly intravenous vitamin C at a local clinic and the Bill Henderson protocol – basically a gluten-free vegan diet plus a cottage cheese and flax seed oil concoction intended to feed her body's healthy cells and starve the cancer.

I poured soy milk into my coffee because they didn't have coconut milk, held the phone between my ear and shoulder. "At least let me fly to Sacramento and meet you," I said. "I'll drive the icy part home with you."

OUTSIDE BAGGAGE CLAIM in Sacramento, I shivered in my sweatshirt while the smokers on the bench behind me complained of global warming.

When Maia pulled up in the big red Oldsmobile that used to belong to Gammie, I felt a sudden nostalgia, like maybe everything was normal again and I was a daughter and a granddaughter and Gammie was picking me up at the airport in Big Red because I'd run out of money in some foreign country and my *I-Ching* had advised me to go home for the deep of Winter and maybe Gammie had agreed to put the ticket on her credit card if I'd pay her back someday. But when I climbed into the passenger's seat, the Oldsmobile didn't smell like new upholstery and Coco Chanel. It smelled like cigarettes. I pretended not to notice. And then there was the more alarming reality: The entire back seat was packed with clothes and shoes, books and knick knacks, lamps and framed art – even a chair. This wasn't a car packed to come home for a week at Christmas. This was a car packed to move home.

"What's up with all your earthly belongings, Maia?"

She pushed a Duke Ellington CD into the player as she pulled out of the airport. I liked that Gammie's old car still traveled with Gammie's old CDs. "I want to be with Nonna," Maia said, matter-of-fact. "I took a leave of absence from school."

I closed my eyes. Surely this was not happening. *Who quits college in the middle of their junior year?*

"You can't drop out–" I tried to muster some maternal authority, like she hadn't already done it, like we weren't already driving north into a blizzard with everything she owned.

"I'm not dropping out, Mom." She said it slowly, like maybe I was getting dim-witted in my late 30s. "I took a *one*-semester leave of absence."

"What about the boyfriend?" I whined. They'd been dating for a couple of years and had just moved in together in a cute apartment in Brentwood.

"He's fine with it," she tried, but now tears streaked her makeup. Her hair was long like always, but she'd dyed it black.

"What's going on, Mai Mai?"

"I can't tell you." She kept her eyes on the highway. And then, "Okay. He's been on a coke bender for two weeks. He hasn't slept. I had to leave."

I thought, *Please, God, no. Really? The boyfriend? But he was so cute*. I thought *Can't he just go to rehab?* I thought, *Good for you, Maia, it took me months to leave my first coke-head boyfriend, but why does he get to keep the apartment*? I said, "Are you serious? What an asshole."

My phone buzzed. *The boyfriend*. I showed Maia the caller ID, but she just shrugged.

"Yes, this is Ariel."

"Yeah? Ariel?" The boyfriend's voice was heavy with exhaustion. "Would you like to know what your *daughter* did now?"

I'd always liked the boyfriend, but my disenchantment was immediate.

"She's gone," he said. "*That's* what. She left. She's probably cavorting around Hollywood with some *guy* or one of her slut friends. How do you like that, *Mama*?"

"Excuse me?" I had to interrupt the boyfriend. "Are you calling me because you're concerned about my daughter's safety or because you want to tattle?"

The boyfriend was silent for a moment. Then, "I just think," he slurred. "I just think you should know where your daughter is."

"Thanks. I actually have a pretty good idea where my daughter is." I clicked the phone off.

Maia rolled her eyes. "Sorry, Mama."

I sighed. "Don't worry about it. Just pull over at the next exit and let me drive."

WE ROLLED BACK onto the highway, Duke Ellington playing "Take the A Train" and "It Don't Mean a Thing," and as we wended north out of the Sacramento Valley and up into the snowbound Cascade range, Maia curled against the passenger side door and fell asleep.

I glanced in the rearview to see how far we'd come, but the piles of all her stuff blocked the window.

IN TIMES OF crisis, I learned as a child, gather bandages and prepare food.

On a bad day when my stepdad had gone to work early, I woke to the shrill screams coming from my sister's room – my mother and Leslie trying to gouge each other's eyes out with the broken shards of a piggy bank, echoes of *I hate you I hate you I hate you*.

It's a way to feign control, I guess, to stay calm and practical, to get up and get dressed in your purple corduroys and your Joan Jett and the Blackhearts T-shirt, to creep barefoot down the hallway and into the kitchen.

My mother and sister would emerge soon enough, bloodied and hungry, Leslie stone-faced angry and my mother laughing. I'd have the herbal antiseptic spray and gauze and

Band-Aids ready for them on the kitchen counter, cinnamon toast crisping in the oven. "Good morning," I'd chirp, like I'd been up for hours and hadn't heard a thing.

NOW I JUST wanted to sit by myself in my own little kitchen, barefoot and writing feminist books and psychology blogs, but somehow I was still wearing my purple corduroys – tending wounds and feeding people.

So it was that on Maia's first full day back home, the house smelled like laundry detergent, garlic, and the fresh bend of a Christmas tree. Four o'clock in the afternoon and it was already dusk. I stood there ironing, making a mental list of the ingredients I had to buy to make the mushroom-leek risotto recipe from the cancer-free newsletter.

Sol would be home in a couple of hours and she'd let the door slam behind her and I'd jump, just a little, afraid of what she might be mad about tonight.

My mother would join us for dinner.

"I'll pick Maxito up from preschool and get a movie," Maia offered. "I'm thinking it's a *Sunset Boulevard* kind of a night."

No matter what happened in our dwindling family, we could always bond over a good Hollywood noir. It was definitely a *Sunset Boulevard* kind of a night.

I COOKED.

We waited.

As Maxito and Maia hooked the last lights onto the tree, my mother floated in an hour late for dinner. "Mai Mai Person, you came home – "

Maia wrapped her arms around her. "Nonna, I've missed you."

Maxito crawled up onto the red couch to be nearer to my mother.

Tonight she wore a black dress and red lipstick, heavy Mexican silver bracelets and necklaces.

My kids wanted to bask in her glow.

She'd always been this way – alluring, like hot metal.

"I'm sure you've heard your grandmother has cancer," she said, her voice suddenly low with the glamour of it.

I should like to die of consumption, Lord Byron once mused. *The ladies would all say, "Look at that poor Byron, how interesting he looks in dying."*

I didn't think my mother wanted to die, but she'd always been drawn to the romance of illness. If she had to die, I knew she'd want to look interesting.

She glanced over her shoulder as if she'd just noticed the tree. "That is the driest, most pitiful excuse for a Christmas tree I have ever seen in my life."

I'd bought it off a Delancey Street Foundation lot and couldn't see what was wrong with it.

"Maybe we like Charlie Brown trees," Maia tried.

Maxito beamed. "I like Linus and Snoopy."

NONE OF US had the nerve – or whatever it might take – to ask my mother about her diagnosis or her thoughts about the coming year, so we waited for her to pipe up.

"Cancer," she informed us at the dinner table, "is a disease of emotional repression." She lifted a glass of wine and half-smiled. "So obviously either I'm the exception – I'm cancer's mistake – I've been unjustly colonized – I'm the Bahamas when Columbus was aiming for India. Or I don't have it. I don't have cancer at all."

Maybe she wasn't going to skip the "denial" stage after all.

"That's interesting," Sol said. "What are you thinking?"

"I'm thinking what I said," my mother snapped, slamming her glass on the table. "Either the doctors have made a cruel mistake or the cancer itself has made a mistake. Everyone knows that people cause their own cancer with negative thinking and I didn't cause this. I've been unjustly invaded."

Sol nodded. "Of course you didn't cause it."

"This isn't my fault," my mother said.

"Of course not," Maia whispered.

I'D TRACED MY mother's illness back to my stepdad's death, to the day she killed him or they were in on it together, but what did I know? I was just doing what we do, telling myself a story in hopes a story would make things better. If my mother had caused her own cancer I wouldn't have to feel vulnerable. That meant it wasn't genetic or environmental. But she was on the other side of new age logic now. She always believed other people caused their cancers, so what was she supposed to believe about her own cancer?

In *Illness as Metaphor*, Susan Sontag warns us off this kind of thinking, saying "scarcely a week passes without a new article announcing to some general public or other the scientific link between cancer and painful feelings. Investigations are cited – most articles refer to the same ones – in which out of, say, several hundred cancer patients, two-thirds or three-fifths report being depressed or unsatisfied with their lives, and having suffered the loss (through death or rejection or separation) of a parent, lover, spouse, or close friend. But it seems likely that of several hundred people who do not have cancer, most would also report depressing emotions and past traumas: this is called the human condition."

So maybe this was just the human condition. Or the human condition with cancer. It was something caused or random, a technological problem to be solved or romanticized.

I did the dishes.

IT FELT A little crazy, this consciously trying to take my hands off the controls, this willingness to follow my dying mother. But it made sense in ways that mattered to me.

It made sense in a Buddhist kind of a way, for one thing, and I was half a Buddhist – philosophically, anyway.

"Anything you're attached to, let it go." That's the advice

the 11th-century Tibetan yogi Machig Labdrön got from her teacher. "Go to the places that scare you."

My mother scared me sometimes.

It made sense to me in a Catholic kind of way, too, and I was half a Catholic. My stepdad had been a Catholic priest before he married my mom. I was never baptized, but I grew up praying favors from Saint Martin de Porres, Saint Christopher, and Our Lady of Perpetual Help. I thought of all those images of the pierced heart of Mary – the seven swords that represent the seven sorrows. But they say those swords aren't the things that cause our wounds. The swords are markers of strength earned through struggle. And the first sword was the Sword of Surrender.

I wanted to surrender.

It all made sense in a spiritualist kind of a way, too. And I was probably part that. I lit a seven-day candle with an image of Marie Laveau on it. The voodoo queen of New Orleans, she was the problem solver. Maybe she could solve all this.

It made sense to me in another way, too, maybe a more important way – a way that didn't have anything to do with spirit or dharma or faith or surrender. And maybe this is the part I shouldn't tell you, because I don't want you to misunderstand. But it made sense to me in a journalistic way. Because more than a Buddhist or a Catholic or a spiritualist or an adult daughter, I'm a journalist. I've been making media about parenting and psychology and women's work all my adult life. I've never been a daily newspaper reporter, but I'm a journalist. And when the wildfire changes direction, threatening a town or when those first shots explode and people with any sense grab their children and their poodles and hurry to evacuate – that's when the journalists come in – rushing toward the storm or the crime scene, not because we're adrenaline junkies, but because we know that something important and human is about to happen. Something true and real even if it's tragic. Something that might require a witness.

Maybe I wasn't the kind of journalist who flew into

hurricanes or civil war zones. (I wanted to be that once, but I always had little kids at home who needed their dinners made). Still, I was a journalist. That's how I understood myself. And the only way I knew how to make sense of my world was to do what journalists do, to rush in and try and dispatch some usable truth from the human places that scare us.

MAIA PUSHED THE *Sunset Boulevard* DVD into the player. That Hollywood gutter at dawn. Dead leaves and scraps, burnt matches, and cigarette butts. The credits, then sirens. That classic shot of the body floating in the pool. The voice-over: "Yes, this is Sunset Boulevard, Los Angeles, California. It's about five o'clock in the morning. That's the Homicide Squad, complete with detectives and newspapermen. A murder has been reported from one of those great big houses in the 10,000 block. You'll read about it in the late editions, I'm sure. You'll get it over your radio and see it on television ... But before you hear it all distorted and blown out of proportion. Before those Hollywood columnists get their hands on it, maybe you would like to hear the facts, the whole truth."

My mother leaned back into the red couch. "You've come to the right party," she mouthed along with the voice over. "You can't beat old Hollywood," she sighed. "Nothing the least bit interesting has happened since film noir."

6. San Quentin

"IT'S IMPERATIVE THAT YOU UNDERSTAND THE NATURE of evil," my mother said. We were driving north through the fog across the Golden Gate Bridge, on our way to visit my mother's boyfriend on death row at San Quentin, Pink Floyd on the cassette player.

I was a teenager. I'd run away and come home a couple of times already.

The last time I ran away my mother was the prison art teacher. Now she was in love with one of the inmates and she cried, "I was fired for love! Blacklisted for love!"

So she wasn't a prison employee anymore. Just a forty-something married woman dragging her teenage daughter to visit her boyfriend on death row at San Quentin and talking about all the things I needed to understand. Evil, for one.

I knew she wasn't talking about the death row inmates when she talked about evil.

We parked in the visitor's lot, ducked into a white building and signed in. We stepped through a metal detector, headed up an asphalt walkway, in through another door.

Wait for that door to close behind you before you open the next door.

The visiting room smelled of stale coffee and cigarette smoke.

And here was my mother's boyfriend, hands folded in his lap and waiting for us.

Next to him was The Midnight Strangler, convicted of raping and murdering maybe a dozen women and children in Los Angeles.

And here was The Midnight Strangler's new fiancée, Doreen. She wore a Gunne Sax dress and too much mascara.

And here was another one of my mother's former students, The Suburban Psycho. He looked like Mr. Clean except he was black. He said he was framed by a prostitute for knifing some white land developer in the cul-de-sacs.

And here was a big white guy with gang tattoos on his neck and my mother pinched his cheeks and cooed at him and he snarled before he smiled.

San Quentin. It all seemed perfectly normal at the time, that we should sit down together at a big plastic table.

I lit a Camel no-filter.

The Suburban Psycho lit a Marlboro.

"Cigarettes are bad for you," someone called from across the room.

"So is cyanide gas," my mother's boyfriend called back from our table.

And everyone laughed like that was the funniest thing.

I wanted to be back in the car with Pink Floyd. I didn't think capital punishment helped anyone, but I wasn't sure death was the worst fate.

My mother nudged me and whispered, "See that man?" She gestured with her chin toward a thirty-something guy with a handlebar mustache. "Do you see that man, Tiniest?"

He wore prison blues and cursed as he pushed vending machine buttons, trying to get a Snickers bar out of the thing.

"That's Bobbie Harris," my mother whispered. "He was literally beaten out of the womb."

I nodded, kept my eye on the man.

"He murdered two teenage boys just to see what it felt like and then he finished their half-eaten hamburgers," my mother whispered. "That's cold-blooded murder. But you have to understand. Bobbie was beaten out of the womb. There's no name for that like *cold-blooded murder,* is there? That's how people get to be like that. Beaten out."

I kept nodding like I understood, like I could understand.

My mother stared at me, wouldn't stop staring.

I felt nervous, didn't want to hold her gaze, so I turned away.

But now The Midnight Strangler was staring at my tits, wouldn't stop staring. He had the darkest brown eyes.

I wasn't sure what to do, so I offered the Midnight Strangler a Camel no-filter.

As he took the cigarette from me, he let his clean fingernails graze the back of my hand.

My throat felt tight.

The Midnight Strangler's new fiancée, Doreen, gave me the stink eye – like I was some teenager moving in on her man.

7.
Clowns and Caregivers

NO ONE THOUGHT I'D GET THE PRICE I WAS ASKING FOR my little house next to the railyard in Portland.

"This neighborhood is all foreclosures," the real estate agent warned me. She had platinum hair and impossibly white teeth. "You've got to be realistic."

Our neighbor across the street shook his head at my flyer. "Dream on," he sighed.

My mother sniffed around the newly beige corners of the place, too. "You'll never sell it. These shades are hideous." She pulled her green Patagonia jacket tight around her like maybe the colors were chilling, too. "I'll *pay* for you to have this professionally repainted. Even a person who knows *nothing* about color is going to have an unconscious reaction to this. It's like a cross between a hospital and a bottomless bog. Anyone with a *soul* who walks in here is going to feel at once ill and trapped."

"Project a little, Mom?"

"Very funny, Tiniest. I'm just trying to help you. I don't know why I bother."

I didn't care. I wasn't going to slash the price or redo the walls. So maybe my house *wouldn't* sell. Then maybe I wouldn't have to move and maybe my mother wouldn't get sick and I wouldn't have to take care of her and then maybe she wouldn't die.

Just because I put a "For Sale" sign in my front yard didn't mean anything had to change, did it?

I buried a Saint Joseph statue next to the sign and the house sold in a week.

Crap.

I rented it back from the new owners.

THE PALE ORANGE to-do list on the fridge:

Pack
Ship
Medicaid paperwork
Write Psychology Today *blog*
Wrap up teaching gig
San Francisco reading March 25
Reno reading April 13
What to do with the cats?

MY MOTHER COMPLAINED that nothing was moving fast enough. "Doesn't anyone understand that I'm dying?" she cried when I stopped by her apartment to drop off a prescription from her naturopath. "I have a *death* sentence. I'll be dead in October." She held a paintbrush in each hand, but had no canvas. Her fingers were just wrapped around those brushes. Her dark red nails dug into her palms.

Everyone had a different idea about when my mother might die, but she marked the date red in her calendar. *October 18, 2010*. Exactly a year from her diagnosis. "I'm running out of time," she said. "I'll be dead on ten-eighteen-ten."

I didn't know about 10/18/10, but I knew had to get her moved while she still had the energy. So that night at my kitchen table the five of us ate spicy yam stew from the cancer-free newsletter and hatched a plan. Maia and my mother would go ahead to New Mexico and get settled into the stucco duplex on the dirt road. I'd fly in and out of San Francisco for my reading, then Maxito and Sol and I would drive down from Portland to Santa Fe via Reno come first blossom of spring.

Maxito played with his noodles on his wooden high chair tray and sang "Wo, Wo, Wo your boat…"

Maia texted someone under the table.

Sol excused herself, saying she had to water the plants in the backyard. She grabbed a lighter off the counter before she stepped outside. Of course we had no plants in the backyard. And it was raining.

I sipped from a glass of sparkling water I'd already spiked with a little gin.

Yes. We were going to do this.

I CHARGED TWO one-way tickets on my emergency credit card and off Maia and my mother flew, their carry-ons stuffed with chalky naturopathic cancer remedies.

SOL AND I bought a 1968 Shasta compact trailer to drag behind our car. We painted it turquoise and stitched red curtains. If things didn't work out with my mother in Santa Fe, well, we could always live in the trailer. *A six-foot by ten foot trailer. What more could three people need?*

AT A CURBSIDE table next to the vegan burrito food cart on Division Street, Maxito picked at his cheese-less quesadilla while Sol and I discussed our situation – the date we had to surrender the house and my interior decorating plans for our little trailer. A twenty-something girl with Little Orphan Annie hair and a red clown nose smiled at us from the next table. People often dressed like clowns in Portland. I didn't know why, but I'd gotten used to it. Finally the clown got up, leaned over Maxito's shoulder to pass us a note. *My Dear Fellow Humans*, it started. *Please excuse the written communication, but I have taken a vow of silence. I couldn't help but overhear your conversation and I know an organization that assists homeless families like your own*. She'd jotted down a phone number and website.

I thought to explain to the clown girl that we weren't homeless exactly, that we were moving and maybe it was complicated, but I just thanked her and she bobbed her head up and down like, "You're welcome," and I loved her even though she was kind of a cliché.

BACK IN JOURNALISM school they taught me that every story needs a "nut graf" – a paragraph that contains those nutshell statistics that will give a universal context to a personal story. Maybe it's a little late in the narrative now, but here's the nut-graf: In any given year, almost 30% of the U.S. population will be caring for an ill, disabled, or aging friend or family member. The caregiver will offer an average of 20 hours a week in unpaid labor and over $5,000 a year in out-of-pocket expenditures. According to some researchers, all these numbers are higher in queer communities. The typical caregiver, it turns out, is me: An adult female with children of her own caring for her widowed mother.

At Powell's City of Books downtown, I picked up a hardcover about "the transformative journey of the caregiver." I scanned a few early passages and learned that the stress of this whole project could take ten years off my life and yet, for some reason, the advice offered at this juncture was to "buy zany gifts" for my mother.

I bought no zany gifts.

Instead I Googled "take ten years off your life" and learned that there are actually lots of ways to do it: smoking, drinking, raiding the fridge, not exercising, eating too many eggs, general pessimism, and motherhood, to name a few. At least I'd be in good company.

IT WAS DEEP winter and the sky dumped frozen rain. Sol and I packed up my mother's apartment on 82nd Avenue, packed up our own house by the railyard and sent everything off with a cut-rate moving service.

I pawned my two cats off onto an aging metrosexual Ken doll look-alike who said he could communicate with them telepathically and would transition them from the lousy generic food I'd been feeding them to an organic raw diet. We'd called them Ricky and Lula since they were kittens, but the Ken doll would call them Atlantis and Lhasa.

"All right," I shrugged.

"They'll be very happy," he promised.

NEWLY CAT-FREE, I sat in my car outside the Ken doll's house. My phone buzzed: Maia. It had been a few days since I'd talked to her. "Hello?"

"Mama? The movers are here." Maia's voice was steady on the phone.

The movers. In Santa Fe already. I fiddled with the radio dial. KBOO was broadcasting an indie music festival.

"Um," Maia said. "Nonna is throwing away your furniture."

I clicked the radio off. "What?"

I could hear my mother screaming in the background: "Don't tell her I'm throwing this crap away, tell her I'm *burning* it."

Maia cleared her throat. "Actually, Mom? She says she's going to burn it. She's piling it all in the backyard. She's making a bonfire."

It occurred to me that my daughter would make a good crisis counselor. Still, I felt something hot in my chest, just under my heart and I thought I might really lose it right then. Break my windshield with my fist at least, let my hand bleed into the drizzle. But I'd been reading my Pema Chödrön books like a good half-Buddhist, so I took a breath instead, focused on the crack in my dashboard. "Why is Nonna burning my furniture?"

"I don't know," Maia sighed. "She says it's all crap. The blue bookshelf, the pink bookshelf, the nightstands. All your stuff, really."

There was a quick rustling sound and now my mother was on the phone, screaming and shaky. "I told you only to bring good things," she coughed. "Just cut me some slack," she said, softly now, like she might be crying. "I have cancer. I have stage four lung cancer."

"Don't worry," I said in the best soothing mama-voice I could manage. "Can you put Maia back on the phone?"

"Hey," Maia whispered.

"Listen. If there's nothing you can do about the furniture, that's fine, but call me back if Nonna starts opening my boxes."

"Okay," Maia promised. "I can make sure that doesn't happen."

Live with me for a year. Then you may ask questions.

I was going to have a lot of questions.

Book Two

Cities of the Interior

8.
Water in the Desert

ON THE MAP IT WAS JUST A PALE BLUE EGG BETWEEN two Nevada towns we'd never heard of, but when we veered off the access road and onto the graveled shoreline, the silvery water glowed like some giant gasoline rainbow, poisonous and beautiful.

How long had we driven in that hazy heat?

A black and red sign at the water's edge warned of unexploded munitions. DANGER: COULD CAUSE SERIOUS INJURY OR DEATH.

Maxito cried, "I want swimming–" He'd been promised swimming.

How do you explain to a two-year-old that some people thought it was a good idea to spend decades testing weapons on a rare desert lake?

Looking out over that poisoned water, it seemed like such a scam of anti-earth abuser culture to teach people that they cause their own cancer with negative thinking. *Maybe this desert lake had been guilty of negative thinking?* I sighed at the meanness of it all. Like lime juice in your eyes to better resemble your colonizer.

WE'D LEFT PORTLAND on a rainy morning. All that lush green and damp gray. Maxito cried from his carseat when the turquoise trailer came off its hitch two blocks from home – the ruthless sound of metal scraping asphalt. But Portland magic appeared in the form of a sleepy hipster who tumbled out of a corner café, calling, "Hey, my grandparents used to have a trailer like that," and "I know just how to hitch it."

We rolled out of town then like every cliché, Sol waxing romantic about the life we'd finally have. Some perfect queer family under the sun.

Driving with Sol, we only listened to her music – to Bowie or Dylan or Freakwater or Steely Dan. The first year we were together she simply pushed eject whenever I chose the CD, so I'd given up. I liked Sol's music well enough, but I wondered what kind of music I might listen to these days if I hadn't spent eight years deferring. It made me sad to think I didn't know what I liked anymore, didn't know what I'd choose.

We drove a couple hundred miles, then spent a snowy night camped at the edge of a little town full of scruffy mullets, Wrangler jeans, and old hippies waiting for the UFOs.

Morning and a couple hundred miles of dotted yellow lines and green highway signs. Portobello mushroom burgers with friends in a Sierra mountain town that smelled of pine. We swam in a river and Sol cried on the rocky bank. Sol always cried at clean water. Her father was on trial for his oil company's genocidal pollution in Latin America. She'd gone to college and veterinary school on the profits of destruction. It was part of the reason she felt morally obliged not to charge people much for her services. Like she was repaying some of her father's karmic debt by tending parakeet wounds.

A couple hundred miles then of cowboy bars and neon-lit brothels and here we were now at this glowing lake and clean water had become a precious thing.

We had to keep going.

IN A CREEPY motel office in a town of old miners' graveyards, there was a napkin-lined basket full of muffins and a Post-It note that read "Martha made these. FREE."

Free muffins, Maxito decided, could almost make up for a

long and waterless day driving. "Muffins," he hummed, swaying in his fuzzy blue pajamas. "I love agua and muffins."

Our room smelled like cigarettes.

Sol read to Maxito from a book about unpolluted rivers and lonely rabbits and the two of them fell asleep on the queen-sized bed. I sat on the toilet because that's where the wi-fi worked. "Dear Nevada," I status-updated on Facebook. "I'm lost." I checked my email.

> **From:** *evedebona@yahoo.com*
> **To:** *arielgore@earthlink.net*
> **Subject:** *Santa Fe*
>
> Tiniest,
>
> I've been trying to call you all day. You're either out of range or you're avoiding me. It is urgent that you contact me. DO NOT COME TO SANTA FE. If you do come, DO NOT PARK YOUR TRAILER ON THE PROPERTY.
>
> Love,
>
> Mom

I READ THE email a couple of times. Surely she was kidding. *Do not come to Santa Fe?* She had to be kidding. She used to call me on April Fools' Day mornings to tell me she'd adopted a giant frog she had to walk on a leash or that she was unexpectedly pregnant with Anderson Cooper's baby. But it was too late for April Fools.

I crept out of the motel room. The warm night smelled like truck exhaust. I stepped back into the free muffin office and asked the man behind the desk to point me to the nearest bar, but he shook his head.

"Nothing like that in this town." He looked like an aging Anthony Perkins from *Psycho* with those dark little eyes and cleft chin.

Do not come to Santa Fe. Sure. Who needed Santa Fe? Why

would we come to Santa Fe? Maybe we could just settle here in this weird little barless town on the edge of a nuclear test site.

I turned to leave the office, but Anthony Perkins called after me. "I'll give you a night cap, little lady." He poured a couple of shots of tequila into two Styrofoam cups, pushed mine across the desk.

I wasn't going to refuse. "Thanks." The drink was warm and rough, but it soothed my throat.

Anthony Perkins winked at me, lit a menthol cigarette. "You know there's a whole army base under that lake, don't you? Yes, Ma'am. You came from the lake didn't you?" He knocked back his tequila, poured us each another Styrofoam shot. "It's a submarine naval training station under there. Good one, huh? The Russians or the Chinese or nobody never gonna suspect a *submarine* base in the middle of the desert, are they? Submarine training in the desert." Anthony Perkins kind of squinted and laughed at the same time. "Is that your sister you're traveling with?" He gestured toward our room with that chin.

"Yeah. My sister." I nodded. "I better get back to my sister."

Anthony Perkins lifted his Styrofoam cup and smiled at me. "To family," he said.

I tapped the edge of my cup against his. "To family."

A couple hundred miles then down the 95 in the already-hot morning, the odd ghost town rising up from the brown-green sand and shrub. Nevada.

I studied my map. Lake Mead wasn't so far. *Surely this blue hawk-shaped thing on the map just outside Vegas would be swimmable.*

AS SOL AND Maxito splashed in Lake Mead, I collected garbage on the shore and dialed Maia's number.

"Hey, Mama," she breathed into the phone.

"Hey, Mai Mai. So, I got this email from Nonna?"

Maia sighed. "Yeah. We were staying at this hotel in Santa

Fe, but we got kicked out. I don't know what Nonna did to them, but the cops came and kicked us out."

In the lake, kids threw their plastic balls and squealed and splashed while their parents drank beer and yelled at them from their beach chairs on the shore.

"What's wrong with the duplex, Mai Mai?"

"Well, Nonna kind of had the house, like, gutted. See, she doesn't want it to be a duplex, so – and, well, she didn't get a building permit or anything, right? So she doesn't want the trailer on the land. Because it might draw attention. Then she'll get fined ten thousand dollars which she doesn't have because, you know, she gave the rest of her money to the contractor and, should I go get her?"

"Yeah, put her on the phone."

I looked across the lake's surface, out past the kids and all the motorboats and water skiers, the brown-red rocks and mountains beyond.

A cool two billion years ago, this was the Western coastline of North America. California and Oregon hadn't yet come crashing in. I thought about continental collisions and inland sea floods, volcanic eruptions and the ash and lava flow that would seal this rock and land together for a while. Now the earth's rift crust stretched to pull itself back apart here, separate continents still desperate to diverge.

"Finally," my mother said by way of *hello*.

"Where I am I supposed to go, Mom? I sold my house. I'm traveling with a toddler here. I can't just *not* come to Santa Fe."

My mother kind of groaned an exhale into the phone. "Ariel, don't get hysterical. I'm going to build us a beautiful home. In the meantime I'm going to rent us a beautiful little guest house. I've just found something on Craigslist. It's small. One room. It sleeps five. The migrant workers of the world would certainly consider it quite luxurious. But, honestly, Ariel, if it's not good enough for you, get your own place. I can't take care of *everyone*. I have cancer."

I didn't know what to say. "Mom, this is insane. That duplex was partly mine. You just ... gutted it?"

My mother hummed. "All right, I'll tell you this, but only because I want you to understand. The contractor and the worker I've hired didn't want this job. The worker is suicidally depressed. He's been through something no one should have to go through. The contractor is bankrupt at nearly age seventy. He's *wonderful*. He has a Ph.D. in Anaïs Nin."

"You're serious, Mom? Anaïs Nin? This qualifies him to take a wrecking ball to the house?"

"Don't be dramatic, Ariel. I hired them both out of self-imposed early retirement. I had to plead with them. These men *need* this project. I may be dying, but I can give these men their *lives* back. Just try to think about somebody other than yourself, Ariel."

I felt like throwing up, but I just closed my eyes. "All right," I said. "I'll do that."

Maybe it wasn't Nevada's fault, but right then I hated Nevada. I stared at it for a long time, Nevada. A few tears fell, but the hot desert air just baked them into my cheeks. There's a color called blue and that's what the sky was. Maxito came bounding out of the water, at first a silhouette against that blue, then into full color with his red swim trunks and green bug-eye goggles. "It's *cold* water, Mama."

Sol stepped up behind him, took one look at me. "What's wrong?"

I shook my head. "Nothing."

THAT NIGHT AT a dark campground picnic table after Maxito had gone to sleep in the trailer, I spelled it out for Sol.

She quietly filled her glass pipe with weed, lit the bowl and breathed it all in. "So the contractor knows a lot about erotica?"

I sipped my whiskey. "Anaïs Nin just wrote erotica to make money. Her major works are – you know – modernist surrealist – like – *Cities of the Interior*. About architectural spaces that don't actually exist."

"Oh." Sol took another hit of weed and nodded. "That don't exist."

JUST A FEW miles in the morning to the Hoover dam and across the Arizona border where they asked Sol for proof of her naturalized citizenship and searched our trailer for human cargo as if Arizona was an independent country and this was an international border.

At a café in Kingman, I put in a few hours teaching my online writing class while Sol and Maxito killed time at a park. I checked Santa Fe Craigslist for housing, found a listing for a quaint little adobe on Canyon Road and called the landlord.

He said, "Sure, come and look."

A couple hundred miles then and a night in a rented teepee. I watched the quarter moon through the smoke hole and I prayed for nothing in particular, prayed that I wasn't right here and now irrevocably ruining Maxito's life, that I wasn't ruining my own.

Just a few months earlier, in Portland, I'd had what I always imagined I wanted: A partner and a home of my own, work in my chosen field, Maia making her way to an undergraduate degree. Some kind of an all in the list of checkmarked boxes I called life. I thought of my Gammie, and the way she'd pour herself a nice, tall vodka tonic whenever she saw my mother enter a room and sip her drink and whisper under her breath, "If there isn't chaos, there soon will be."

Weak morning coffee and a couple hundred miles and the highway sign read *Welcome to the Land of Enchantment*. Casinos, desert, heat. A mid-spring dust storm held the highway in a terracotta haze.

Do not come to Santa Fe. When we got there, I didn't want to stop at the gutted house, didn't want to tell Maia or my mother we'd arrived. So we just sped past the duplex that maybe wasn't a duplex anymore. It didn't look any different than it had back in November when I flew down and made the offer on it. Flat roof, faux-adobe stucco walls. A long rectangle of a place set on the property at an odd angle, as if it had landed there accidentally. A few dented pickup trucks were parked in the driveway, but no other evidence hinted at demolition or construction.

We drove down Old Santa Fe Trail and up the hill to Canyon Road to look at that quaint adobe. The landlord had said "sure, come and look," but when we pulled up with that turquoise trailer, two road-tired and tattooed queers and their sugar-faced kid, well, that landlord came running out and yelling into the street. "Do you know where you are?"

I didn't know.

"It's Canyon Road," Sol whispered.

"So?" I was confused.

"This is the center of the art trade in all of America," the landlord screamed. "This is the *Wall Street* of Santa Fe!"

I didn't quite know what he meant by all that, except that we wouldn't be renting any quaint little adobe.

The landlord was white like me but he called after us: "I am one of the premiere Native art dealers in the world!" And he shook this creepy wooden doll at us like a warning.

I squinted at Sol as we drove away. "This is the Land of Enchantment?"

We checked into the Econo Lodge, into a room next to the indoor pool.

"Swimming," I whispered to Maxito.

And his tired face lit up.

"Come on." I took his sweaty hand.

Outside the picture windows, the Santa Fe sunset painted things orange and we all sank into the chlorinated blue. Just three travelers. Submarine training in the desert.

9.
What If I Lived Here?

DO YOU EVER PLAY THAT GAME "WHAT IF I LIVED HERE?" You're just driving through some bright city or rain-washed town. *What if I lived here? What if I lived in that pink trailer off the interstate? Or in that little brick house near the university? What if I lived in that giant glass spaceship of a building that clings to the Pacific sea cliff? In that apartment with the picture window and the fire escape? In that ugly development at the state border? In that purple houseboat? Or here?*

I OPENED MY eyes and stared up at the cottage cheese ceiling. *Where was I?* It took me a long minute to put it together. Econo Lodge, Santa Fe. *What if I lived in Santa Fe?*

I'd always played "What if I lived here?" but I'd always kept on driving.

What would be the next step in the game? Geographical roulette. What if I gave myself 24 hours to build a life in this town where I knew almost no one? Then I'd call Maia and my mom and admit that we'd arrived.

I left Sol and Maxito sleeping and headed down to the motel lobby for my promised "deluxe continental breakfast," a stale bagel. I sat at a round table, clicking around on Craigslist looking for a life. There were houses and apartments that required full year leases, overpriced vacation sublets, and "ideal for one or two adults." People who wanted to discriminate against kids were always so blatant about it.

I clicked on commercial rentals. Sol and I had been self-employed in Portland, would be self-employed in Santa Fe. Maybe I'd find a place where I could teach writing workshops and Sol could run a little veterinary practice. We'd talked about opening a candle shop, too. And here was this: *Santa Fe's pioneering live/work rental community now leasing*. I clicked on the floor plan. We'd get a 400-square-foot studio apartment, a storefront downstairs, and a back room – all for less than our mortgage back in Portland. This could be our life.

I woke Sol to tell her where I was going.

Maxito slept clutching a big pink hippo from Ikea.

"Sound reasonable?" I whispered.

Sol nodded sleepy. "Reasonable as anything."

Out in the parking lot behind the Econo Lodge, I unhitched the turquoise trailer. I stopped at the Goodwill a mile down to buy clothes that would hide my tattoos, but the hiding was hardly necessary. The landlord stood up to shake my hand, sat back down behind his glass desk. A white-haired Midwestern-type with a turquoise belt buckle, he had that mellow out-West vibe.

I scribbled the rental application.

He glanced over it. "Where you from, Ariel?"

"California," I said. "Originally."

He nodded without looking up. "What part?"

"Bay Area. Born on the Monterey Peninsula."

He nodded again, leaned back in his desk chair and thought about that. "You know, it's funny," he said. "I used to know a Gore down on the Monterey Peninsula. I did. In the sixties. You ever know a Jim Gore?"

I didn't know if it would help or hurt my chance at the rental, but I blurted the truth. "Sure. He's my biological father." It wasn't every day I met someone who'd ever known my schizy dad. He lived in Thailand now, collected butterflies and disability.

"Far out," the landlord said. He gazed out his sliding glass doors at the lavender and sage that exploded from the planter boxes outside. He didn't ask if my biological father was still alive or how he was doing, just mumbled "I dropped a lot of acid with Jim Gore." He pushed a lease across the desk for me to sign, shook his head. "Far, far out."

IN SANTA FE there were no tall buildings, just the flat-roofed adobes and fake adobes, the low mountains of the Sangre de Cristo range always in view. Every strip mall consisted of exactly one nail salon, one burrito shop, and one store featuring some very specific item made from organic cotton. Downtown add turquoise and silver, green chile and arugula, galleries of sunsets, and "contemporary tribal."

I DIDN'T WANT to go see my mother in her rented casita, didn't want to tell her we'd arrived or that we wouldn't be moving into any single room with her. I just wanted to think about the random new life I was building as if it were a driving game. I wanted to imagine a world in which my acid-dropping father and my mirror-gazing mother had never decided it was a good idea to get together and breed. Would the universe have given me different parents? Or would I still be an unrealized notion in the firmament? I just wanted to sit in my car next to my trailer in the Econo Lodge parking lot and watch the day's dust storm roll in from the north.

My phone buzzed. A message from my mother. Just the address of her casita and *you might as well stop by and say hello*. She already knew we were here.

Of course she knew.

A FEW HOURS later, Sol and Maxito and I stepped into the one-room casita that smelled of Paloma Picasso perfume. My mother didn't look up from the little wooden table. She just fawned over blueprints and fed cucumber sandwiches to an older man I figured was the Anaïs Nin contractor. They sipped red wine in the dusty afternoon and threw their heads back and laughed.

"I'll need a chef's kitchen," my mother was saying.

The man doodled something onto his plans. "You'll need the best stonemason in New Mexico to redo that fireplace," he said. He was good looking in that aging scholar who never landed a professorship kind of a way; he wore a wedding band.

"I'll need a complete water purification system," my mother said. "Not to mention an air purification system."

The man kept adding marks to his plans. "You'll need the best cabinet maker in the Southwest."

My mother swooned and refilled his wine glass. "Well, hello." She glanced up like she'd just noticed the three of us standing there inside the doorway. "Look at what the cat dragged in." And then, "Oh, Ariel, don't make that pitiful face. I'm joking, obviously. This is Ronaldo. Isn't he marvelous?"

The Anaïs Nin contractor crossed his arms over his chest. *Did he just wink at us?* "Ronald," he said. "And your mother is the one who's marvelous."

I nodded. "She's something, isn't she?"

My mother had only been living in the casita for a couple of days, but the watercolor Henry Miller painted for her in the '60s hung on the wall. She sighed, placed her hand on her contractor's shoulder. "Ronaldo never actually *met* Anaïs Nin."

Ronald smiled a too-wide smile and raised his little eyebrows. "You know, Anaïs was a sexual revolutionary, so some people refer to her as the first hippie," he explained without being asked. "Nothing could be further from the truth. She was, in fact, the last modernist. The hippies didn't understand her."

"The last modernist," my mother hummed.

It made my skin crawl to imagine what this creep was thinking. My terminal mother pretending to be wealthy. Anyone could see that she was beautiful, but Ronald had to be starstruck, too. If my mother was an old lover of Henry Miller's, well, that made her just one lover removed from Anaïs Nin. It practically *made her* Anaïs Nin. He'd found the very last modernist. And maybe she was loaded.

I glanced over at Sol. She just shook her head and whispered, "We're fucked."

I looked down at Maxito. Two years old and all love and acceptance, but he stared at his grandmother and this new man now like even he was starting to feel confused and desperate. "Hungry," is all he said.

"Well, anyway, my little urchin progeny," my mother sighed, waving her hand toward the contractor's plans and then toward us. "The house is going to be beautiful. I'll make any deal I have to with God or the Devil to let me finish it before I die."

The afternoon sun angled in, giving my mother a sudden otherworldly glow.

It kind of blew my mind how she could be so bizarre and so textbook at the same time. Elisabeth Kübler-Ross' third emotional stage after a terminal diagnosis: Bargaining. You fill your calendar, you start a major project, you extend your deadlines, you make your deal, you buy time.

AS WE WALKED back out to the car, my phone rang. *My sister.* I handed the keys to Sol, buckled Maxito into his seat. "Hey, Leslie."

"Hey, dude. Mom emailed that her contractor has a Ph.D. in Anaïs Nin."

"We just met him. Total creep. And it's a Winchester Mystery House moment over here." That old California Victorian had been under constant construction for almost four decades because the widow who lived there thought if she finished it, she'd die. Finally it was a hundred and sixty rooms and a mess of stairs that led nowhere and doors that opened to blank walls. She ended the construction. And died.

I heard the flick of Leslie's lighter and her quick inhale. "Winchester Mystery House meets *Henry and June*," she laughed. "Whatever. Listen. Tell Mom that I hate Santa Fe with a passion and I wouldn't come visit her there even if she was the last mother on earth. Not even if she builds a giant haunted house."

I kind of wanted to slap Leslie through the phone, but I

just said, "All right. I'll make sure and tell her that as soon as possible."

Leslie cackled just the way my mother did. "Is there anything I can help you with from here?"

"Not really. Thanks for asking." I clicked the phone off, glanced out the car window. Another strip mall: Nail salon, burrito shop, organic cotton dog clothes.

Santa Fe. I lived here now.

10.
Conquest

THE SOUND OF DRILLS AND THE SMELL OF FRESH PAINT. We were turning that gray live/work space into a bright candle shop/veterinary clinic/writing studio at trainspeed. With a little bit of profit from selling your beiged-up house by the train tracks and a Home Depot credit card, it turns out you can build a quick life anywhere you like.

We moved what was left of our belongings – carloads of clothes and the furniture my mother hadn't burned – into the studio apartment and a storage unit down the street.

I bought New Mexican cookbooks from Collected Works Bookstore and shopped for the ingredients at Sunflower Market. Blue corn flour, pinto beans, and red and green chile – I could feed my little family on the cheap here.

Everything was sunshine and transience.

Maia had found a job at a shoe store at the mall, was saving up to get herself back to Los Angeles and college in time for summer session. She showed up at the half-finished live/work space her first day off wearing baggy jeans and high-heeled boots and we put Maxito's car seat in the back of the Oldsmobile and left Sol to paint things blue and the three of us drove off over a speed bump to pretend this new life was something normal.

At the farmer's market at the railyard we stocked up on kale and apricots, green chile mustard and red chile raspberry jam. Maxito tapped his foot, tried to sing along with the one-man band – a bejangled old guy who played his accordion and twanged Loretta Lynn and Drifters songs.

"Santa Fe is cute," Maia promised. "When I first got here I was like, *Why have I even heard of this town? It's nowhere.* But it's all right."

ALL OVER TOWN, plaques and monuments bragged that Santa Fe was the oldest capital city in the United States, the oldest European city west of the Mississippi, home of the oldest public building and the oldest community celebration – a merry autumn fiesta commemorating colonialism and reconquest. We laughed at the signs. They may as well have just said, *Eat it, New England*. The streets had names like Avenida Cristóbal Colón and Paseo de la Conquistadora.

Maia had hoped to convince my mother to come with us to the hot springs an hour out of town, but my mother said she didn't have time. Maia shrugged. "Who needs miraculous healing waters when you can shop for tile with Ronaldo?"

No matter. I was happy to spend the day alone with my two kids who hardly ever got to spend a day together.

We drove the old highway south out of town, listening to the Native radio station that played songs about dusty dashboards and expired tags. Maxito pointed out cactuses and giant birds as we cruised through half-ghost towns with their abandoned mines and their Old West art and anarchy. We circled back north, past the casinos and the sandstone rock formations, through the towns full of double-wides with low riders and old luxury sedans parked out front.

We crossed the Rio Grande and then the Chama, those red-brown rivers still rushing from the spring's late snowfalls.

The three of us had never been some idyllic family in a soft-focus Sears portrait, but I appreciated the ease of no-held-breath in Gammie's old car, no insults and nothing burning. Just Maia driving, Maxito babbling his Spanglish and counting cacti from the back seat, and me watching out the window, that desert highway dotted with cemeteries and wooden crosses decorated with plastic flowers.

We got to Ojo Caliente in the blue heat of afternoon and Maia and I took turns soaking in the arsenic tubs and playing with Maxito in the lithium swimming pool where he was allowed to float and laugh far away from the relaxing yuppies with their eye pillows.

"These are our Native waters," a woman in the lithium pool was saying. Her grandson bobbed up and down next to her. "It's offensive that these white people from San Francisco with their Kokopelli tattoos claim to 'own' it. They charge us twenty dollars to get in and tell us we can't bring our children?"

Her friend sat poolside, feet grazing the water's surface. She pointed her middle finger toward the main office behind us. "Kokopelli this, bitches."

We laughed, and it all seemed so normal – this world of blatant conquest and rebellious submission.

Maxito stuck his face in the water and blew bubbles.

"It's beautiful here, isn't it?" Maia whispered as she approached.

It was. Beautiful.

Afternoon faded into evening and Maia took Maxito into the restaurant for a buffalo burger while I soaked the last of the day away alone in the arsenic tub, watching the cliff swallows dart overhead while stars began to appear, at first one by one, all bright and quiet in the darkening sky, then as if by the hundreds.

IT SEEMED IMPOSSIBLE, how many stars. I held my breath and wished on the falling ones and almost thought that something important and holy was about to happen to us. Almost had the nerve to hope. But right there on the verge of hope I felt the muscles around my heart contract and I felt something more like panic. All those stars.

11. Trends in Bleeding and Dying

AFTER THE LAST SNOW FALL IN MAY AND BEFORE THE monsoons of early summer, Maia repacked the big red Oldsmobile with all her earthly belongings and headed west to her new studio apartment in Pasadena to catch up on her junior year.

My mother had commandeered the turquoise trailer and was living in it out behind the gutted duplex. She complained that Ronaldo was slow and an asshole to boot; complained that a mountain lion came down from the hills in the evenings and paced outside the trailer door. "A sham of a contractor," she sighed, "and a lioness stalking me."

Sol and I opened our candle shop/veterinary clinic/writing studio on a bright Tuesday and I guess there wasn't much else going on in Santa Fe that week because the newspaper ran a huge color photo of us on the front page of the metro section and people stopped by to pick up their seven-day Guadalupe candles and their Saint Christopher car statues and their blue glass evil eye beads. They stopped by to find out if Doc Sol could cure their dog's ragweed allergies, stopped by to ask about memoir workshops and announce "I've always been told I should write a book."

In between customers I worked on editing projects and Sol studied rodent anatomy books. Maxito had just started a new Spanish-immersion preschool and it seemed like we might win this game after all. *What if we lived here?* Look at us manifesting a life out of stardust and panic.

A poet I'd once heard of stopped by the blue shop to introduce herself. "I saw you in the newspaper," she said. "I've read your books." She had long, dark hair that was just beginning to gray, wore peacock-feather earrings. "Ariel?" She cocked her head to the side. "Do you know that you're bleeding?"

At first I thought she was talking metaphorically, the way poets do, but I'd been bleeding a lot since we got to Santa Fe. Nose bleeds, ear bleeds. I hadn't been particularly accident-prone back in Portland or California, but here I cut my fingers and stubbed my toes. Here I tripped on jagged stones and ripped my skin. I grabbed a tissue from under the counter, held it to my nose.

The poet looked worried for me. "Be careful," she said. "The desert wants your blood. I'll live here all my life, but I won't die here. I don't want to be buried here. Not in the desert. The star beings are waiting."

I nodded like I understood.

"Believe me or don't," the poet said. "I'm Indigenous and Italian, so I'm a witch on both sides."

"I believe you," I promised. "Do you mind watching the shop for a minute? I need some coffee."

Sol had ducked out for a miming class.

IN THE CAFE across the street, I noticed the barista had raw wounds on her wrist like she'd been cutting herself.

"Oh, yeah," she said when she noticed my tissue, "the bleeding." She had gothic script and a few stars tattooed on her neck. "If you don't let the blood on purpose, you'll bleed when you least expect it. The only way to stop it is to harvest an elk."

"An elk?"

There were paintings of crescent moons and adobe houses on the café walls. Santa Fe paintings.

"Yeah," the barista said. "You eat the elk's organs. Raw." She pushed my soymilk latte across the counter. "I mean, if you want to stay here and not bleed."

I grabbed my latte and nodded like I might actually do it – harvest an elk. *I mean, why not?*

I'D AGREED TO meet with my mother and a hospice intake nurse at the shop that afternoon. My mother still didn't need much in terms of care, but I was trying to make the calls friends told me I should make, trying to plan for a future I didn't understand. I figured our first day open at the shop would be slow. So just after the poet left on that bright Tuesday, a fifty-something woman dressed in pink came ballet-stepping in through the French doors.

I leaned across the counter to chit-chat with our pink hospice fairy, explained that my mother really didn't have many symptoms, but she did have this diagnosis and I was trying to get ready for we-didn't-know-what.

"You never can be too ready," the intake nurse chirped. She had fuzzy blonde hair and a fuzzy rose-colored sweater. "How wonderful for your mother that she has you, Ariel. It's going to be quite a journey." She leaned toward me and whispered, "One thing to watch out for is when she starts coughing up blood. Promise me that you'll call us when she starts coughing up blood."

"Sure." I didn't ask if she expected my mother to start coughing up blood without warning or what. I just nodded. "Of course I'll call."

A CUSTOMER STEPPED in. "Greetings from the north, south, east, and west – " She wore flowing sage linens and amber jewelry. She reached her arms out like a scarecrow – or maybe like a crucified person. "Ah," she said, turning her palms upward. "I know and feel that I am in the right place. My co-worker has placed a curse on me. Do you perform curse reversals?"

"No," I had to admit. "I do not personally perform curse reversals. But I have a Marie Laveau candle here if you're interested. She's the problem solver. Or you could try Santa Barbara. She's known for her protective qualities."

The hospice lady squinted at me, like *are you a witch or what?*

The cursed customer spun around three times, grabbed both candles, dropped a ten-dollar bill on the counter, and rushed out, calling over her shoulder "blessings and thank you from each of the four directions."

"Any time," I called after her.

The pink hospice lady scanned the candle shelves for just a few minutes before my mother crept in looking particularly pale and tired.

It occurred to me that maybe my mother could just turn this illness thing on and off at will – transmutation at her fingertips. Snap and she could be misdiagnosed or terminal, seductress or victim, abusive mother or old woman in need.

The pink hospice lady whispered, "She's beautiful."

I'd brought three folding chairs out from the back room, but the hospice lady dragged the giant Mexican equipale chair from the corner of the shop, like maybe she thought it looked more comfortable than the folding chairs. She motioned for my mother to sit down in it, but when my mother did sit, the image was all wrong, my tiny mother in that giant pigskin chair. She was maybe 95 pounds now, but she looked even smaller in that ridiculous chair, feet not touching the floor. Lily Tomlin as aging cancer patient.

The hospice lady didn't seem to notice. She and I sat in our folding chairs and she shrugged and smiled, shrugged and smiled. "People are really into conscious dying right now."

Who knew there were trends even in dying?

"I don't want to know anything about dying," my mother said.

"You don't want to know?" The intake nurse smiled a wide white smile like she'd never heard such a thing, but she was going to be nice, like some preschool teacher pretending that sucking on one's own knees might be in the realm of the socially acceptable. "It's important to be conscious as you decline," she tried.

"I'm not declining," my mother said. She inspected her manicure.

"Are you in pain?" The hospice lady asked.

"No," my mother said. She sucked in her cheeks and looked more gaunt.

"Because if you're in pain we can help you with that, Eve. We're here to help you. Whatever you need. As you know, you've been automatically admitted to hospice because of your diagnosis and your lack of insurance outside Medicare and here we are to help, help, help. You might not be in pain now, but as you decline you'll be in bone-crushing pain, Eve. I mean bone-crushing. *Conscious, conscious.* At this point we'll just come and visit you from time to time. You'll meet your nurses. You'll love those little gals. Now, are you sleeping well enough, Eve?"

"Yes," my mother said.

"About how many hours each night?"

"Five. Maybe six hours. I worry."

I didn't pipe up. Maia had mentioned that when they were staying in the casita my mother slept two, maybe three hours a night.

"We can give you something for that," the pink hospice lady offered.

My little mother in her giant chair. She rolled her eyes. "I would never take your medication."

The hospice intake nurse nodded, unfazed. "Are you into alternatives?"

"Yes," my mother monotoned. "Alternatives."

"Well," the pink lady smiled. "Here's the alternative, Eve. Every evening – every single evening just before sunset – you go outside and you bathe your eyes in the sun. You bathe them, do you understand? It's called sun gazing. Have you heard of it, dear? It's ancient. You *gaze* at the sun. Every evening, Eve. Do you hear me? Every single evening. That will cure your insomnia and, well, you never know what else it might cure." The pink hospice lady with her fuzzy hair giggled. "Those ancient Egyptians knew a thing or two about immortality."

When the hospice lady finally stood up and placed her hands on her pink hips and said, "We *are* here to ferry you to the other side, my beautiful little sun-gazing Eve," and smiled wide and side-stepped out the door and let it close behind her, my mother looked at me with a mixture of terror and trying-not-to-laugh and she said, "Ariel, you are *not* allowed to parody this."

12. Curses

OUR CANDLE SHOP HAD BEEN OPEN A MONTH THE DAY a white girl with dreadlocks ducked in. "Are you Ariel?"

"I am."

She smiled, already pleased with herself. One of her front teeth was broken in half. "Well, well," she said. "I just thought you should know. Your girlfriend, Sol, is leaving notes for Bipa at the mime school."

"Excuse me?"

"You know the master mime? Bipa?"

"Sure," I shrugged like I couldn't care. "I know who she is. I didn't realize she still lived in Santa Fe."

"Yeah," the dread girl said brightly. "Bipa moved back here last fall. She lives in that earthship at the edge of town." She looked around at all the candles like she'd just noticed them. "Cute shop. Well, good luck."

Santa Fe suddenly felt small like that, everyone hungry for some fresh morsel of gossip or betrayal.

"Thanks?"

But the dread girl was already gone.

Bipa.

Amy Winehouse sang from the iPod behind me.

I picked up the phone, called the café across the street and ordered a soymilk latte and a pile of enchiladas without cheese. Maybe I just needed some calories and some caffeine.

"Red or green chile?" the barista on the phone wanted to know.

"Christmas."

"You got it, honey."

I recognized her voice. The girl with the neck tattoos. But it was one of the waiters who stepped into the shop ten minutes later with my plate of enchiladas. "I could use your help," he whispered as he set the plate on the counter. "My girlfriend. She may be cursed." He had smooth skin and a boyish smile.

I hated to think his girlfriend was cursed. Hated to have him believing that. "Why do you think that, Amador?"

He looked over his shoulders, made sure we were alone. "I can't get her pregnant," he confessed. "She really wants to get pregnant. Do you have a candle for that?"

I pointed him to the hummingbird candles. "Light that pink one. She could also try acupuncture."

Days at the shop were like that. Just waiting to see who'd come in next and what they might want or need.

THE DOOR OPENED. A woman with gray hair walked in carrying a cardboard box, set it on the counter in front of me. "Will you sell these candles I made?" She took a seven-day candle from her box. Onto the glass holder, she'd glued an interesting color Xerox collage of an old witch in front of her house on chicken feet. "Are you acquainted with Baba Yaga?" the woman asked. She had a little bit of a mustache.

"Sure," I said. "The old hag who flies around in her mortar kidnapping children?"

The woman with the mustache frowned. "Dear goddess, Baba Yaga is much more than *that*. She helps people on their quests. She inhabits the worlds of both life and death. She offers guidance to lost young souls. Think of the old Russian story *Vasilisa the Wise*. Of course Baba Yaga requires that Vasilisa works for her, serves the irrational, sorts the poppy seeds from the dirt, prepare her feasts – but Vasilisa completed her tasks without asking too many questions, without asking the wrong questions, and she was rewarded with light and wisdom. Vasilisa got a better life.

"All right," I said. "I'll take a dozen."

"You won't be disappointed," the woman promised as I forked over twenty four bucks.

THE DOOR OPENED again. My landlord. He wanted the rent.

No problem.

So I was sitting there eating my enchiladas with Christmas and writing the check to my landlord when my mother threw open the French doors.

When my landlord looked up at her in intricately embroidered Mexican cottons, his mouth kind of fell open.

"Ariel? As loath as I am to admit it," my mother announced. "I may owe you an apology."

I couldn't recall my mother ever apologizing to anyone for anything. But who knew? Maybe my mother was experiencing some late-life transformation. "How do you figure?" I asked.

My landlord stared at her. Here was my mother, the very last modernist turned frail old woman.

She looked into him.

His hair was white, too. He wore a bolo tie. "Is that you, Eve?"

She cocked her head to the side. "Are you?"

He nodded slowly. "Far, far out."

I pushed the rent check toward him, closer to the edge of the counter, wanted him to take it.

One of my creative writing teachers used to say that when an object passes between two people in a story, you should slow the narrative down because it's more than an object passing between them, it's energy.

But before I could slow down the narrative, my landlord pocketed that check and scurried out of my shop like some so-busted teenager.

My mother bowed her head and whispered, "That man dropped a lot of acid with your father in the sixties."

I nodded. "I've heard."

My mother looked disoriented for a moment, then refocused. "I'm too tired to stand, Ariel. Don't you have a chair?"

I pointed her to the too-big Mexican equipale in the corner and she collapsed into it. "Nobody knows how sick I am," she sighed. She shook her head, then started to cry. "Nobody knows how scared I am, Ariel. All I'm asking is that you do what you said you'd do." She buried her face in her small manicured hands, then straightened her back, seemed to compose herself. She stood up, stepped to the glass counter and leaned across it toward me. "Tiniest, I'm only asking that you come and live with me and help me even the *slightest* bit. I don't ask very much, do I? I have stage four cancer. I'll be dead in a few months. I don't want to be any trouble, Ariel. I've spoken to a Jungian analyst about all of this and he tells me you're angry about your childhood and that's why you're abandoning me and, Ariel, I'm sorry about that. I would take that on if I had the strength. But your need for revenge is more than I can handle right now. Please just let that go and help me?"

My heart went out to her. It always did. But I didn't know what to say. Maybe it would be a good time to explain my point of view? Lyle Lovett was singing on the player behind me and my mother seemed authentic in her pleading rant. I stood up straight. It seemed important to have good posture when trying to confront my dying mother. "I sold my house," I started. "I packed up my family. I came here. When I was en route, you emailed me not to come. But, see, I'd already sold my house. When we got here, the duplex we'd bought together wasn't a duplex anymore. And it wasn't inhabitable. I couldn't even park my trailer outside because you didn't get a building permit. I have to say–I'm having the hardest time seeing all of this as my abandonment of you."

I swallowed hard.

"God." My mother flung her head toward the counter like she was really going to bash her forehead into the glass, but she stopped just short, straightened back up, looked me in the eye. She had dark eyeliner tattooed on. "Ariel," she said gravely. "I cannot *believe* you're 40 years old and you're going to make this about you. Fine. I'll give you the name of the analyst. I'll stop seeing him myself. Will that make you happy? Get some much-needed analysis? That's fine. Just move in. We'll have a functional kitchen at some point. In the meantime there's a perfectly good camping stove in the backyard. One of the bathrooms is now enterable. You know how loathe I am to ask you for anything, but pitifully, Tiniest, you're all I have." She took a piece of paper out of her purse, unfolded it and placed it on the counter next to the evil eye beads. It was a Xeroxed picture of a generic female body and it had red dots of various sizes drawn on it; a doctor's name in the corner. She pushed it across the counter. The moment when I'm supposed to slow the narrative down. "These are the tumors," my mother said. "These are the lung tumors we already knew about." She pointed to the red dots around the Xeroxed figure's lungs. She pointed to the red dots in the figure's liver. "But it's metastasized to the liver, and," she pointed to the figure's head. "The brain." She looked at me now, placed her finger on her left eyebrow. "I have a brain tumor. I can feel it from the outside. Touch it?"

I didn't touch it.

"Ariel, as hard as this is for me to say, I would love to be allowed to share my last dying months with Maxito. If you insist on bringing that control freak, Sol, well, fine. It's just a couple of months. This is *all* I'm asking of you."

She shook her head when I didn't answer. "Why don't the three of you just come over to the house tonight. We'll watch *Dark Passage*, the Humphrey Bogart and Lauren Bacall film."

"All right," I agreed. "Sure."

But I already knew we were sunk for more than movie night.

13.
Lung Cancer Noir

TWO MONTHS SHY OF THE DEATH DATE MY MOTHER HAD written on her calendar in red pen, Sol and I sublet our studio apartment to an art student for the school year. We'd keep the shop space downstairs.

"Your situation is interesting," the art student said as he signed the lease agreement. "If there's a gay kid in the family, it's always the gay kid who has to take care of the sick parent. I always thought that was because the gay kid wouldn't have any children of their own. But that's obviously not true for you."

I shrugged. "Always great to be the gay kid." And we packed up the car again for our move across town.

"Let's make a pact," Sol said as she turned the key in the ignition. "If we start plotting to murder your mother, we have to move out."

I laughed. "Agreed." But I knew she wasn't kidding.

THE HOUSE WASN'T a duplex anymore, but my mother's now-master bedroom was separated from our smaller bedrooms by the dining room, living room, and the huge unusable kitchen.

Our first weeks in the house, I focused on cooking. On the camping stove in the backyard, I made calabacitas, ancho and mild green chile stew. When the doorbell rang and my mother spied one of the hospice nurses, she hissed in my ear: "It's one of those maidens of death. Send her away."

We moved here to "help," but what could we do? Our joint

tasks included shopping for organic groceries and cooking when my mother was home, not asking where she was going when she left, and being polite to Ronald, who came and went at odd hours carrying expensive building supplies and appliances he didn't seem to know how to install.

"I'm here with electrical wire," he announced one night after dark. He had a key to the front door. "Anyone know how to wire a place?"

My solo tasks included paying all the bills, keeping track of my mother's alternative healer appointments, and making sure there was a steady stream of Netflix noirs coming to the mailbox.

Sol, for her part, was to make herself available to move heavy furniture from one end of the house to the other and back again whenever my mother screamed her name.

I STUMBLED ALL the time. I couldn't feel my feet on the ground. I didn't take my contact lenses out even at night, didn't want to get caught off guard.

And then one day a bird fell from the eaves in the front of the house. A dead bird on the cement walkway just before the front door. I didn't think much of that first dead bird, but they kept falling. Every week, then every few days, then every day. Dead birds, covered with ants when I found them.

I was afraid the dead birds would spook my mother, so I scooped them up with the little garden shovel and buried them in a secret bird cemetery in the backyard.

Packing the dirt over their graves, I thought about the lover I had when I was eighteen – he was twice my age. He'd choke me just until I gasped, bite me just hard enough to break the skin. I was inexperienced and turned on and confused. I'd never heard of all that – the ravenous pleasure at the brink of violence. What could it mean?

"Do you like it?" my lover whispered in the dark.

"Yes," I admitted, but I thought there was something wrong

with me – something wrong with my brain. At least it had to be anti-feminist. Some patriarchal trap.

"No, baby," my lover whispered as he tied my wrists together. "It's punk rock."

But one night he came home late to the apartment where we slept on the hardwood floor and he started kicking me with his steel-toed boot and when I screamed he yelled, "I thought you liked that, bitch," and kept kicking.

Did I?

Like it?

I gasp-groaned as I heard the ribs snap; as I tasted blood.

"Do you like that?" he slurred. He was just a shadow above me now and where was I? And who?

"No," I managed. I didn't. Like it. But it was a weak kind of a no. A broken-rib kind of a no. And then it all stopped and there was no sound and no boot and my lover slumped into the salvaged orange armchair in the corner of the room and mumbled, "You *know* you like it."

That was a long time ago now. More than twenty years. I felt my still-uneven ribs under my shirt as I walked away from the secret bird cemetery and I wondered at all the ways abuse invents us.

"DID YOU ALWAYS have a problem with those birds?" I asked the previous owner of the duplex when I saw him in the produce aisle at Healthy Wealthy. He was wearing spandex bike shorts. "Falling from their nests onto the walkway every day?"

He bagged his butternut squash, "I always loved the birds," he hummed. "With their nests in the trees and in the eaves. I can't remember any falling. Maybe though. Maybe once," he said as he walked away.

RONALD'S WORKER, JULIO, cried over the bathroom sink. He was one of the men my mother saved from early retirement. He'd lost his only child in a drunk driving accident and I found him there late one afternoon, just crying. "My daughter is dead and my wife is married to someone else and all I want is a loving family around me and Eve has exactly that and she can't see it."

My mother was standing silent out in the hall and heard him say that, so Julio wasn't allowed in the house anymore and the workers who came after that only spoke Spanish and they didn't cry in the bathroom.

She counted the days to October 18, 2010 and said, "I'll be dead in seven weeks."

Then, "I'll be dead in thirty three days."

"I'll be dead in three weeks. That's twenty one days, you know?"

"I'll be dead this time next week."

Her voice was always monotone and I didn't know how to answer her, so I just shook my head and said, "No. You're doing good, Mom. You're doing really well."

I WANTED TO make sense of these days, but filled my journal with unconnected notes.

8/30/10
Been here two weeks. Not going well.

9/15/10
I ask Mom if she's talked to Leslie and she says "I'm done with your sister."

My biological father finds out that I'm here taking care of her and he emails pictures of naked nurses with enormous breasts. He probably would have posted them on my Facebook page, but he got banned from Facebook last month for inappropriate status updates.

Leslie texts: I am so ready for both those parental freaks to die.

9/27/10
My mom's getting so skinny. She only eats a few bites.

10/11/10
There's no way she'll be dead in a week unless she's planning to blow her brains out.

10/13/10
She doesn't sleep

10/16/10
I'm tired.

10/17/10
In Paris, Alice B. took care of everything. Gertrude just had to be the genius. All her energy and time – just to be a genius. Sometimes I think, seriously? I'm a genius. Where's my Alice B.? I have to move boxes, call hospice, pay the bills, pay Maia's college tuition, take Maxito to preschool, note my mother's new symptoms. Who's going to take care of me? When do I get to be a genius?

ON THE MORNING my mother thought she would die, she marched out into the living room in her leopard-print robe.

I was sipping black coffee.

"Get a load of this," she said as she handed me a print out of an email from Leslie. "For the record, I just told your older sister as *nicely* and as *rationally* as I could that I thought she ought go back to college and finish her B.A. in *anything* or come and live with us here. Excuse me, but what is she doing with her life? And look at this. This is the thanks I get?"

From: *Leslie Gore*
Date: *October 18, 2010 10:21:53 AM PDT*
To: *Eve De Bona <evedebona@yahoo.com>*
Subject: *Re: reality, limitations, options ...*

Dear Mom,

When I said "never bring it up again" I meant just that. I am never going back to college and I am never moving to that godforsaken high desert.

You are a broken record.

Stop telling everyone what they ought to do and what they ought to want and listen for a change.

If you want to see me, buy a ticket, if you don't want to see me, never mind, I would probably need six months of therapy to get over your abuse anyways.

See you in the next lifetime.

Love,

Leslie

"In the next lifetime?" my mother said gravely. She pointed to the brain tumor under her eyebrow.

I texted my sister: *I can't believe you just contracted for another lifetime. I'm so done with her after this one.*

THAT NIGHT, I dreamed of the mountain lion I'd never seen. The lion paced around the yard, slept, waited. I tried to scare the lion away through the windows. I told Maxito and Sol to keep the doors closed so it couldn't get in, but the lion came and went as she pleased through the dog door in the laundry room. No one seemed afraid. We all knew the lion was just looking for my mother. And my mother wasn't home.

I opened my eyes in the dark of bedroom. Sol snored softly next to me and my mother's silhouette was in the doorway waving a giant kitchen knife over her head. I nudged Sol, but she didn't wake. Maxito's room was across the hall. I felt a familiar calm kind of panic, racked my brain for what I was supposed to do or say next to make sure nobody died tonight. Surely my mother didn't want me to laugh. Not now. Or did she? "What are you doing, Mom?"

The clock that glowed green from my nightstand told me it was just after 3 a.m.

"Look what I found," my mother whispered. She held the knife by its wooden handle and it glinted, a little, in the moonlight. "In my new *dishwasher*." She hummed a few lines from "The Sounds of Silence" and grabbed the tip of the knife with her free hand, moved the blade against her throat. "Knives like this don't go in the dishwasher. Do they, Tiniest?"

I was careful to move very slowly as I got out of bed. "Of course the knife doesn't go in the dishwasher." I moved closer to her, kept my voice low and calm. "I don't know how it got there. It was a mistake. Give me the knife?" I held out my hand for it.

My mother glared at me. "You wish I were dead." She pressed the blade into her throat now.

"I don't wish you were dead, Mom. Give me the knife. I'll wash it properly in the sink. With organic soap."

She narrowed her eyes, turned the tip of the knife toward me now, pointed it at my chest, but held it steady a half-inch from my skin. Nobody likes the tip of the knife pointed into her chest, but relief flooded my veins: I recognized that look on my mother's face. Just a glimmer of bright behind her eyes. I knew what I was supposed to do. I laughed. So she wouldn't stab me.

"C'mon, give me the knife, Mom."

She smiled wide, showing the one dead tooth on the right side, stepped back as she loosened her grip on the handle and let me take the knife. "Wouldn't it be funny," she laughed. "If I was that crazy?" She smiled as she backed away, kept smiling and backing away.

Her figure disappeared and then her shadow disappeared. I poked my head into Maxito's room to make sure he was still alive, watched the rise and fall of his chest in the light of the half moon.

In the morning, three dead birds huddled frozen on the front step.

The cold season was coming.

And I worried I wouldn't be able to keep up with all the birds that needed burying.

14. The Water's Edge

SOME MORNINGS WHEN I WAS A KID I WOKE IN THE DARK of my single bed, my mother curled into my back. Shadowy memories of metal in muted light kicked around my mind – fresh images of my mother's manicured hand wrapped around a giant keyring, jagged with all those steel keys and slamming it into my stepdad's forehead until it bled.

"Tiniest?" My mother would whisper. "Did you have any bad dreams?"

I pretended to be asleep because I liked the warmth of my mother next to me.

"Tiniest?" she'd whisper again, and she'd scratch my shoulders lightly with those red fingernails.

"No," I'd answer finally. "I can't remember any dreams."

"Okay, Tiniest." She'd slip out of my bed then, floorboards creaking.

When the door clicked shut behind her, I'd climb out of bed too, pull on my corduroys and Keds, my hand-me-down *Charlie's Angels* T-shirt and I'd crank my bedroom window open silent as I could and slip out.

I'd walk my bike quiet over the oak leaves, then jump on and ride fast, the amber streetlights glowing as the dawn sky began to blue.

Some mornings I saw Michelle Miller's mom getting into her Volvo station wagon for her long commute to the Livermore Labs where she made warheads. "What are you doing out this early?" she'd call as I sped towards her. "Be careful," she'd shout as I whizzed past.

I wasn't afraid.

I could ride that blue three-speed faster than anyone could ride or run and I knew every alleyway and shortcut in our town.

I peddled faster, imagining some helpless shadow chasing after me. I sailed across University Avenue, ditched down another alley and turned onto the bike path that lead down to San Francisquito creek.

Breathless and elated, I threw my bike down at the creek's edge and tossed stones across the shallow water as the first commuter train crossed that old train bridge, *chclack, chclack, chclack*.

WHEN I GOT home, the house would still be quiet.

Only my stepdad up.

I'd creep into the kitchen and say, "Good morning, John."

He'd smile at me and say, "Well, good morning, chickadee."

And I'd pretend I didn't notice the bandages on his head as he fried me a plateful of sliced bananas and leftover brown rice and we'd sit there at the butcher block table, the two of us, pouring honey over our bananas and rice and spooning all that soft sweet sticky mess into our mouths and we'd laugh and lick our lips because we shared this unspoken grateful feeling between us that, yes, we'd made it to breakfast just fine.

15.
Bell, Book and Candle

SUNRISE HELD THE FORMER DUPLEX IN SILENCE.

Maybe things would chill out now that my mother's red ink death date had passed.

Maxito peered around the doorframe into the living room where I was curled up on the couch. "Watch *Bell, Book and Candle,* Mama?" He'd just turned three and this was his favorite film – the Jimmy Stewart and Kim Novak neo-noir about a pretty witch who owns a magic shop and puts a love spell on her unsuspecting neighbor. Maxito played the DVD over and over, laughed at the same blue flame and Siamese cat spell scenes again and again.

"Sure." There was time for a movie before shopkeeping and preschool.

On the camping stove in the cold blue-sky backyard, I made strong coffee and hot cocoa, scrambled eggs with green chile.

Seven a.m. and my mother hadn't yet emerged from her room at the far end of the house.

Eight a.m.

Eight-thirty.

Maybe she was dead in there.

I didn't want to check.

Sol steamed coconut milk for more coffee. "Have you seen your mom since yesterday?"

"No," I lied. "I'm sure she's fine."

I didn't know if the cure for my life was to lie to everyone about everything or to become brutally honest.

"How ARE you?" acquaintances would ask when I ran into them at the Tune-Up Café on Hickox. I'd order my Salvadoran plate, nod and say, "I'm fine and great to see you."

"How IS your mother?" they'd ask when I ran into them at Healthy Wealthy. I'd place her probiotic cottage cheese and organic shiitake mushrooms in my cart and say, "she's doing all right."

I didn't want to say too much to anyone about my mother in part because I'd been taught since childhood not to. My stepdad and my Gammie and the few friends who knew the quality of her violence said she couldn't help the way she was and anyway, *Come on, Ariel, she's tiny, who could she hurt?* And I didn't want to say too much because, inexplicably, I still wanted people to like her. I was afraid they wouldn't like her. And then my new acquaintances would be like every mop-haired hippie kid I went to elementary school with in the '70s in California, those kids who used to slap my head when I passed them in the hallways and say, "Hey, Airbrain Ariel, how's your bitchy mom?" Bitchy because she'd called them a corporate greedy sugar dealer when they just wanted to sell her a box of Girl Scout cookies. Or bitchy because she'd followed them home after they broke a bottle in the street and she'd grabbed them by their shirt collar and told them to "come back, you little brat, and clean it up. I work at San Quentin – that's where thugs like you end up." Those kids friended me on Facebook now and wrote on my timeline, "I always admired your mother and I'm so sorry to hear she's ill," and I kind of wanted to slap their heads.

NINE O'CLOCK IN the morning and my mother finally emerged from her bedroom in her leopard-print robe and a Patagonia jacket.

"Nonna –" Maxito beamed when he saw her. "*Bell, Book and Candle!* Want to see the funny part?"

My mother smiled at him and sighed, "Good morning, Maxito." But when she turned to me she wasn't smiling anymore. "Why haven't you put the grandmother clock together?"

"I haven't had a chance," I said. And I hadn't – consumed as I'd been about whether or not she'd try to murder my child as I slept. "There's hot water in the backyard for your essiac tea. Do you want me to bring it inside?"

She nodded slowly. "If you were planning on staying here you would have put the clock together by now. You're going to leave me here alone to die, aren't you?"

I didn't want to leave her alone, but how much longer could we stay? "We'll have to figure something out that works for everyone. Okay?"

I checked my email. I'd applied for a sweet visiting professor gig at the University of New Mexico and here came the good news: Unanimous vote. I was hired. I'd start mid-January.

Who was I? A mother, a daughter, a professor.

The snow would be coming soon.

I HAD FANTASIES of running away like I was 16 years old again. Maxito and Sol and I would pack up our lives into three little backpacks and we'd climb out the window and run laughing into the cold night.

But we didn't run.

Instead I rigged baby gates in the hallway that led to our bedrooms and told my mother I'd done it because I worried about Maxito sleepwalking.

THANKSGIVING CAME AND we could finally use the kitchen even though it still needed paint and countertops. We roasted the requisite turkey even though no one but Maxito and Ronaldo was eating meat that week.

CHRISTMAS AND MY mother said the tree I'd brought inside was even more pitiful than last year's and, "I'm trying to be tolerant, Ariel, because obviously you don't have any money, but get that fucking thing out of my house."

I left it where it was.

Maia flew in for the week and tried to get us all drunk on mescal and shivered, "It's stressful here."

I wrapped a couple of candles from the shop and put them under the tree for my mother.

She gave me a can of smoked sardines.

THE DAY AFTER New Year's I lit a Virgin of Guadalupe candle, but I didn't know what to pray for. Maybe God had enough trouble without worrying what happened to us.

Sol took Maxito to a circus-themed party somewhere at sunset.

I paged through an unlabeled file on the kitchen counter. New Xeroxed figures with my mother's name on them. New tumors in the lungs. New tumors in the brain. A new tumor the hospice nurse had circled in red pencil: The one that pressed into the mitral valve, beginning to cut off the blood supply to her heart.

"How are you doing?" I asked her when she shuffled into the kitchen.

She put a pot of water on to boil. "I'm dying, I'm sure you're happy to know." And then, "I don't know what your family is doing here in my house."

I didn't know what to say. *Your family. My house.* I was tired of this shit, tired of making excuses for her, tired of blaming the tumors or anything else. And it wasn't true that she couldn't help the way she was. She didn't treat everyone this way. She was just an abusive bitch who happened to have cancer. I shook my head, looked right at her. "If anyone in your life has ever treated you like family, it's been me and my kids. If you can't see that, take it up with God."

As I turned away, I heard her low whisper, "You just made a big mistake."

I crawled into bed even though the sliver of a moon had barely risen. I thought I'd read or write, but I just took a few good sips of bourbon from the bottle on my nightstand and fell asleep. Didn't wake when Sol and Maxito came in.

IN THE MORNING, I made coffee and hot cocoa. I scrambled an egg for Maxito. I didn't see my mother. Didn't hear her in her room. Didn't hear the laundry running. We took Maxito to preschool and went to work at the shop, but it was cold and snowy and no one came in so we closed early, picked Maxito up from preschool early and headed home.

As we turned onto the dirt road, Sol gasped, "What the mother?"

Twenty seven giant black garbage bags in the driveway, our red couch behind them. The grandmother clock. My old hobo bird painting propped against the turquoise trailer.

"Watch *Bell, Book and Candle* again!" Maxito cheered from his car seat.

"Hang on, Maxito." Sol pulled over and I climbed out of the car, blast of cold air and the sound of my own boots on the gravel. I tried the front door, but the front door was locked. My key didn't work. That's when I noticed the living room windows were all boarded up. I walked around the side of the house. My mother's bedroom window was the only one not boarded. It was open and there she was in her green Patagonia jacket, just staring out the window, the screen between us.

"What's going on, Mom?"

She kept staring like I wasn't standing there on the other side.

"Mom, what are you going to do?"

She was quiet at first, didn't move except to smile at a question like that. "Don't worry about me," she finally said. "The devil takes care of his own."

SOL WAS LOADING bags and cursing under her breath when I got back to the car. Maxito whimpered in his seat.

"Don't worry, baby." I whispered. "It's just a game. House bounce."

He didn't look soothed exactly, but he stopped crying. "House bounce?"

What was there to do? We couldn't kick the art student tenant out of our apartment on a moment's notice. We'd given him a nine-month lease. And so it was that the three of us, a veterinarian, a professor, and their three-year-old kid moved into the back room of a candle shop best known for the curse-reversals we did not perform.

A short trek through a frozen outdoor passageway lead to the toilet and sink we shared with the Buddhist temple that had moved into an adjacent live/work space. We'd worry about where to shower later.

WE DRAGGED GARBAGE bags in from the car and Sol borrowed a truck from the pizza shop across the parking lot and went back for the couch and clock. I set up the DVD player. "*Mary Poppins* or *Bell, Book and Candle*?"

"*Bell, Book and Candle!*" Maxito squealed.

"We're going to live in our shop now," I told him like it was as ordinary a place to live as anywhere. "Just like in *Bell, Book and Candle*."

"Yes," he smiled. "We live in our shop."

It was dark by the time Sol had moved the couch and the rest of our stuff in. "We need wine," she said.

We did. "I'll go."

She held up a full pink petticoat tutu she'd found in one of the big garbage bags of our belongings. It was mine. The kind of thing people wore in Portland with a pair of motorcycle boots. The kind of thing no one ever wore in Santa Fe with anything for any reason.

"I dare you to wear this to Healthy Wealthy," Sol laughed. "I'll pay for the wine if you wear it."

SO, THAT'S HOW I found myself in the wine aisle at Healthy Wealthy – a mother, a daughter, a new visiting professor, not exactly homeless, wearing my full pink petticoat tutu on a January night in Santa Fe, New Mexico, even though it was only seven degrees outside.

16.
The Smell of Death

WINE-TIPSY IN THE DARK OF OUR SHOP WHILE MAXITO and Sol slept, I clicked onto Facebook. My mother had updated her profile to show that she no longer had any children. I unfriended her, then felt like a worm. *Did I really just unfriend my dying mother?* I poured myself another glass and typed a rambling status update.

My old friend Teagan commented, *Geez, talk about our parents having no use for us the minute we're not who they trained us to be.*

I LOOKED AT my old hobo birds painting propped against the wall, looked out the window. The dark of the new moon. I didn't want to sleep with Sol on the red couch in the back room, so I curled up in the giant Mexican equipale chair in the corner of the shop and fell asleep in my pink tutu like some kindergartener who'd just projectile vomited at the talent show.

Morning was a ringing phone in the pocket of my hoodie. *Hospice*. I'd left a voicemail telling them my mother was alone and asking them to check on her more often, but I guess the fuzzy intake nurse was also the fuzzy exit nurse, because it was her voice on the phone now saying, "Well, hello there, dear Ariel. I'm calling to let you know that well – as luck would have it – your mother fired hospice yesterday."

I sat up in the equipale, tried to smooth my tutu. "She fired hospice?" *Who fires hospice? Hospice is free. When you don't want to see them, you just don't open the door.* I must have been silent for a long minute.

"Ariel?" the intake/exit nurse tried. "Are you all right, dear? May I be frank with you, Ariel?"

"Frank?"

Sol poked her head in from the back room, whispered, "Coffee?"

I nodded. *Please.*

"Yes, dear," the hospice lady was saying. "You want to be conscious as your mother declines, don't you?"

I wasn't sure I wanted to be conscious, but I said, "Sure."

"Well, my little Ariel," the nurse started, her voice all sing-song. "I've been in this conscious dying business for a long time and I'll tell you that most people, when they're dying, want to pull everyone they love in close and just hug 'em tight. But there is a notable minority of people who need to be alone. It may well be that your mother will die alone, Ariel. I think you would be wise to prepare yourself for that possibility. Six weeks or one year from now, a worker or a delivery person or a neighbor will knock on your mother's door and your mother won't answer the door. That worker or delivery person or neighbor will smell that distinct odor of death and they will call the police and your mother will have died. You'll get a call from the police. I think you would be very wise to prepare yourself for that call."

I didn't ask the fuzzy hospice lady with her sing-songy voice how one might prepare oneself for that call. I just said, "Oh." I said, "Well, thanks." I said, "Take care."

Sol brought me coffee in a red mug. "Is everything all right?"

"It's fine."

WE PUT A note on the shop door that said, "By appointment only." Sol would sell the candles and make house calls. I'd wake in the predawn and train-commute to the university to teach the college kids how to invent improbable stories. On those still dark mornings as I walked along the tracks to the train station, I told myself that I didn't have a mother anymore. But I still flinched every time my cellphone buzzed. The call I didn't know how to prepare for. The smell of death.

"You did your best," someone on Facebook said.

But had I?

Done my best?

I felt like a failure.

LATE AFTERNOONS, THE train home from Albuquerque barreled through desolate reservation after desolate reservation and a voice over the loudspeaker announced that we weren't allowed to take pictures of what was left of Native land.

NIGHTS HOME AT the shop we cooked on the old camping stove we grabbed from my mother's backyard.

What was I doing here?

Living with my mother had been its own nightmare, but in that duplex that wasn't a duplex anymore, at least Sol and I had been united in our oppression. Our problem was my mother and whatever piece of furniture she was screaming for Sol to move. Now I was the only one for Sol to glare at. She lingered at the mime school until she had to pick Maxito up from preschool. She announced that she would no longer accept money for veterinary services, that she would only work for trade – it was a matter of principle and pet health.

I rolled my eyes. "Chicken eggs and free massages aren't going to cut it as your family contribution."

But Sol didn't like when I talked to her that way. She crossed her arms and stomped her feet and didn't say anything. I hated the silence, so I went and bought her a piece of cake from the Chocolate Maven and I said I was sorry and I leaned into her and she patted me on the back and kissed me on the head and whispered, "It's all right."

I crept into the front of the shop to grade papers, lit a Baba Yaga candle.

SATURDAY MORNING MY cellphone buzzed with a local number I didn't recognize.

Could it be the cops already? Had someone reported the smell of death?

"Hello?"

"Is this Ariel Gore?" The voice was deep with the softest Texas twang.

"Yes?" I felt a stabbing pain behind my chest bone.

But it wasn't the police. "Ms. Gore? I'm a family mediator and attorney here in Santa Fe. I specialize in child abuse and neglect. I'm calling about Maximilian."

Lump like a piece of hot coal in my throat. My first terror, of course, is that something has happened to him, but I glance back and he's right there on the red couch laughing at *Bell, Book and Candle,* a bunny mug full of hot cocoa on the table in front of him. But maybe something had happened to him we didn't know about? "Yes?"

"I'm calling on behalf of your mother," the voice said. "She's worried about Maximilian."

I swallowed hard, took a good breath and let it go. "He's doing well," I said. "He's well taken care of." I glanced over at him. His perfect skin. His steady smile.

"All right," the voice said. "Well, your mother would like to have visitation with Maximilian once a week. She would like you to bring him to the house to do art. She would not like you to bring Sol. She would like you to go to the house alone with Maximilian."

I felt nauseous, but I didn't want to give this guy anything. I knew enough about family mediators and family court attorneys. I'd spent seven years in a protracted custody and visitation battle with Maia's dad back in California. She was grown now and he was long dead, but I still woke some nights in the cold sweat terror of that courtroom. No, you don't give these guys anything. I said, "I'll have to think about that."

He didn't say anything. I put a Nina Simone CD on the

player behind the counter. Maybe Nina Simone could walk me through this. But as soon as Nina Simone started in, Sol appeared and pressed eject, put Johnny Cash on instead. "Well," the voice on the phone said. "It's within your mother's rights to file suit for legal visitation. If she's concerned about her grandson's well-being, we will of course feel obligated to make a report to Protective Services about abuse or neglect. I understand that you don't have immediate access to a full bathroom ..."

I didn't think the voice was finished talking, but I was finished listening. "I see," is all I said. I clicked the phone off, closed my eyes, and for the first time I prayed, "God, please just let her die already."

LIVE WITH ME *for a year. Then you may ask questions*. That's what my oracle had said. But Sol was the one who picked up the phone in the front of the shop when it rang later that morning, and Sol didn't ask any questions. All I heard her say was, "Eve, don't ever call here again."

Book Three

Underground

17. Blindfold

"YOUR PROBLEM IS THAT YOU DON'T TRUST ANYBODY," the girl in Albuquerque said as she fastened the blindfold over my eyes.

I didn't think that was my problem exactly, but I was going along with it because she was cute and the way she'd always flirted with me on the commuter train made me feel like everything that was wrong with me and Sol was just wrong with Sol.

I'd missed the 5:34 evening train on purpose because I'd glanced behind me and knew she was going to miss it. We were at the bottom of the cement stairs on Central Avenue, cold wind against my face.

The girl in Albuquerque. Girl/woman. She must have been at least 35, but she dressed like a skater boy in her baggy jeans and faded black T-shirt. I wanted to know her name. She had coffee-colored skin, wore silver stud earrings, her eyebrows plucked into thin arches.

That's all I asked – her name – and she didn't answer me and that's when she pulled out the blindfold and said, "May I?" and turned me around and told me what she thought my problem was. Trust. Not trusting anybody.

Now the girl in Albuquerque was pushing me down Central Avenue and I was blind-tripping forward. She turned me against the wind and then turned me around, pushed my back against a cold brick wall and nudged the blindfold off and leaned in to kiss me, her breath hot on my cheek. She had the prettiest brown eyes.

"I can't," I whispered.

"Can't?" she raised those thin eyebrows. "You think I didn't just see you miss that train on purpose?"

It hadn't occurred to me that she might have seen me. Trust. "I have a girlfriend who wouldn't like it."

The girl in Albuquerque smiled at me. Her teeth were bright white and crooked. "And does your girlfriend still kiss you?"

I wished I was 21 or a bigger liar or somehow otherwise only partially responsible for my actions – for what might happen on a windy night in an alleyway in Albuquerque. I wished it badly.

The girl in Albuquerque was still close to me, still held me against the bricks. "Your girlfriend just owns you like that? Outright? It's a waste." She pushed me just a little harder against the wall. "I'm stronger than you," she whispered.

I glanced at the curve of her bicep. "I can see that."

"But I can take no for an answer."

And I said, "Thank you."

But now the girl in Albuquerque looked like she might cry. Thin, arched eyebrows. She said, "Why you got to thank somebody for acting right?"

I didn't say anything.

"Don't ever do that again. Thank me for doing something sweet for you." She let go of me. "Don't ever thank anybody for acting right."

"Okay."

She stared at me for a long time. "Promise."

And I said, "All right. I promise."

The wind and the bricks. All that cold felt like elation and I didn't know what it meant, but something in my life had broken open. I trusted the girl in Albuquerque completely.

Strangers in alleyways had never really been my problem.

I GOT HOME to the shop late. The smell of onions and garlic frying on the camping stove. Maxito already asleep. Sol had made vegan tacos with Soyrizo and kept them warm.

She lit a candle.

"I got paid," I told her. Enough to cover first, last and deposit on a cheap rental.

I knew it wasn't illegal or neglectful to have a kid and share a bathroom with a bunch of Buddhists, but days in the shop had become all anxiety, waiting to see if Protective Services would come and investigate, waiting for a process server to appear with family court papers. Or maybe it would be my mother in the doorway waving her giant kitchen knife.

I would have just as soon moved back to Portland, but Sol wouldn't hear of it. "The only good that's come of all this is we got to New Mexico," she whined.

So I sat with my plate of Soyrizo tacos, scrolled through rentals on Craigslist. Apartments in Santa Fe, houses in Albuquerque, trailers in the old mining town out Highway 14 and this: *Rural and private*. Click. A little adobe with its iron gate and turquoise-painted window sills. Nine hundred dollars a month. Twenty minutes out of town. A third of an acre. Room for the trailer and a trampoline and chickens if we wanted them. A place to hide and mend. A place to make macaroni and cheese and green chile stew. I already knew we would live there.

Saturday morning we drove out to the place, south on the freeway and a mile down the kind of road no one would drive down unless they lived there. Inside the house was all thick walls and tiles, vigas and skylights. *Yes, thanks, we'll take it.* I handed over my first month's visiting professor's pay.

I CHANGED MY phone number and texted Leslie: *If you talk to Mom, tell her I got a job at Lewis and Clark and moved back to Portland.*

I updated my Facebook profile to show that I lived in Los Angeles.

When our acid-dropping live/work landlord asked where we were going, I told him, "New York."

I felt like a fugitive on the lam.

Was I really doing all this to avoid my 90-pound dying mother?

Well, yes. Yes I was.

18.
A Place to Hide

I'D UNLOADED A COUPLE OF BOXES AT OUR NEW LITTLE adobe when a tall tie-dyed fellow in a cowboy hat sauntered into our yard wanting to know where I'd come from and why.

"Just need to lay low for a while," I told him.

He nodded. Evidently, that was the right answer around here. "I live up the road," he said. "You can call me Tex." He had an underground bunker, he said, "For when the shit hits the fan." He scratched his beard. "I have a kind of a sixth sense about people. I can tell if somebody's friend or foe and you're friend, I can sense that, so you just scramble on up to my place and I'll hide you in my bunker if it comes to that." He winked at me. "Just because you're paranoid don't mean they're not comin' after you."

Yes. This was the place for us.

THE SINGLE MOTHER who lived around the corner took a few more days to appear, skittish, on my porch. She wore an Adidas running suit, said she'd noticed Sol building a chicken coop in the backyard and did we have chickens?

"Not yet," I told her, "but we have chicken dreams."

She squinted at me. "Are you Ariel Gore?"

I felt a sudden panic at being found. "Yes?"

But she wasn't a process server. "Oh my God – Ariel Gore. I've read all your books. You look just like your author photos. I thought you lived in Los Angeles."

"No," I confessed. "I live here right now. But, you know, I'm trying to lay low."

She nodded, held my gaze. "Me, too," she whispered. "An ex-husband situation."

"I understand," I promised. "Say no more."

INSIDE, I TOOK a random book from the shelf. I needed a new oracle. *All Things Are Labor* by Katherine Arnoldi. I fingered the gray cover and asked, "What am I doing here?" I opened to a random page, pointed to the middle and read, "What we are looking for is something small that we can use. This is all we need, a little bit, something that happened by chance, something common like a broken piece of glass, some string, a book of matches: just a small thing where there is nothing but what is here to find."

My oracle. I didn't know what it meant, exactly. Except that I should pay attention.

THE LOCAL NEWSPAPERS called that winter mild even though it was the coldest of my life. Cold and easy. The snow glittered, dusting our little adobe as we settled in.

The first dawn of spring came and Sol bought baby chicks from San Marcos Feed Store out on Highway 14.

Maxito squealed as he fed them under their heat lamp. "My chickies getting so big."

Sol drove me to the train station every morning and Maxito to preschool.

The girl I'd let blindfold me in Albuquerque winked at me from her seat across the aisle.

I winked back. But I never missed the 5:34 train again.

In my advanced fiction workshop at the university, we discussed the elements of story. Alexandre Dumas said that to make a novel, you need a passion and four walls. To make a passion, Wallace Stegner added, "you need people in a bind, a situation full of love, hate, ambition, longing, some tension that cries out to be resolved."

What cried out to be resolved here?

This was supposed to be a book about a typical caregiver – a daughter with children of her own trying to help her terminal if eccentric widow-mother through a final year. But now here we were mid-narrative, more than a year gone by, and no one had died and I didn't have a mother anymore and the semester was wrapping up.

Soon I wouldn't have a job.

SOL BROUGHT MY coffee out onto the front porch at sunrise, set it on the low table. "Do you think you'll ever see your mother again?"

I leaned back into the big equipale chair and it creaked the way it did. It seemed like a crass question, but maybe a reasonable one. "I guess not," I said.

Sol sipped her coffee. "How do you think we'll find out when she's dead?"

I didn't know how we'd find out. "We'll find out," I said. "Everyone loves to spread news of death."

My cellphone buzzed just then and I cringed the way I always cringed then, but it was just Abra, a 20-something acquaintance from Portland, texting to say *I'm moving to Santa Fe to go to the Native Arts College, If you still have that trailer, can I rent it?*

I texted Abra back: *Sure.*

SO ABRA MOVED into the six-by-ten turquoise trailer. She was just a few days out of the hospital with a new type 1 diabetes diagnosis, but she smiled bright like any kid getting ready to start college. Over coffee on the dusty porch, she pushed her hair out of her face, looked at us and around, out across the high-desert street and beyond to the naked hills and she said, "Aren't we the Californian, Dominican, Native Alaskan diabetic, gay-straight alliance? I hope there aren't any neo-Nazis out here."

So many people to hide from.

19.
The Fires

THE WILDFIRES CAME MEAN THAT YEAR. THEY STARTED in May and burned into summer. We watched the mountains and the hills around us catch and blaze. The smoke billowed, held heavy in the air. We coughed and bled. More than a hundred thousand acres burned, were still burning. I dreamed of lungs without bodies that glowed red like the fire-season moon and I woke to mornings covered in layers of white ash.

Brown bears and bobcats from the burned out wilderness wandered the streets near our little adobe and we had to keep our chickens inside the house.

The fires tore through pueblos and towns and national monuments. We listened to the radio and TV news reports online. The fires were within ten miles of Los Alamos National Labs.

Within five miles.

Within a mile.

Within yards.

How many yards?

The laboratory PR guy wore a yellow tie and promised, "No threat to public safety," but the professors on NPR warned of nuclear disaster and 30,000 above-ground barrels of plutonium-contaminated waste that would soon catch fire and burst, sending plumes of radioactive smoke into the winds.

As the birds flew, we lived twelve miles from Los Alamos National Labs.

I wanted to evacuate. I packed the car with enough water

and canned food and tortillas for a week; packed all our passports and birth certificates. But which way would we drive? The horizon burned in every direction.

THAT NIGHT, SOL and I invited all the lesbians and trans guys we knew in Santa Fe to come out to our place in the country for vegan tacos. We wanted to pretend we were building community here instead of waiting for all that smoke to bleed radioactivity. And they came – the brave ones came – miles closer to the fires and miles closer to the labs. We fed them tacos and fennel salad and we made small talk and Sol put on a Dolly Parton CD and without announcement all the lesbians whipped off their shirts and they ran outside and the trans guys ran after them and Sol looked surprised, but she whipped off her shirt too and she ran after them all and they chanted for rain.

I watched from my kitchen window and rolled my eyes. It was just so California circa 1970 to 1999. I mean, I didn't know any trans guys back then – but the rest of it.

Abra watched, too, bewildered from her trailer.

They ran unembarrassed, ran the circumference of our property, all those lesbians in their bouncing red bras and the trans guys in their white muscle T-shirts, and they chanted "Rain goddesses! Rain goddesses!" until Maxito couldn't contain himself and despite my obvious disdain, ran with them chanting, "Rain goddesses! Rain goddesses!" and they ran and chanted and ran and chanted until of course the desert winds shifted and the smoky sky crowded itself with monsoon clouds and "Rain goddesses! Rain goddesses!" those clouds opened and the lesbians and the trans guys and Maxito cheered, "Rain goddesses!" and they laughed as the downpour drenched their hair and there would be no nuclear disaster in New Mexico that summer.

No.

There would be rain.

20.
Mime Wave

"CAN I ASK YOU SOMETHING?"

Sol looked up from the Walter Mosley mystery she was reading in bed. "What?"

"When we moved to New Mexico, did you know that Bipa lived here?"

Sol blinked, looked down at her book. "Sure. I knew she'd moved back."

I fiddled with my Gammie's ruby engagement ring I wore on my right hand. "Are you pursuing her? Bipa?"

Sol closed her book "What kind of question is that? That's completely irrational."

I climbed into bed next to her. "Sorry."

She rolled over, curled her back to me. "I've been completely honest with you about Bipa," she said to the wall. "Bipa broke my heart a long time ago. I'm over her."

I SPENT THE balance of the summer and the tip of autumn baking pies in my adobe kitchen, building Lego sets with Maxito and catching flights between Albuquerque and Los Angeles. I'd found work as a ghostwriter. I slept on the leopard-print couch in Maia's studio apartment in Pasadena. I'd bought that couch when I was her age, a single mom with a toddler. Now the two of us stayed up nights eating ramen and drinking strong tea, Maia doing her graphic design homework and me writing in voices not my own. It reminded me of being in my 20s, when we were an easy family of two.

At home with Sol in New Mexico, things teetered between silent irritation and resigned tolerance. This was my life. A little adobe. It wasn't so bad. *Make the best of it, Ariel.*

I was rushing to a departure gate at LAX on my way back to that life when my phone buzzed with a text message from Vivian in Portland: *Just broke up with my girlfriend.*

I texted her right back: *Jealous.*

But then I felt like a cad. Maybe I could fix this thing with Sol after all. I was good at fixing things. We'd been together for ten years. Ten years wasn't nothing. We got along all right when she wasn't mad at me for being three minutes late or for not properly pre-sorting the recycling. She'd never waved a knife at me in the middle of the night or kicked me as I slept. I'd buy her a cake at the Chocolate Maven when I got home. I'd pick a bouquet of wildflowers. I'd find cheap tickets online for a wintertime week in New Orleans. Right before Mardi Gras – when all the bands are practicing in the streets, but before the drunk boys arrive for the party.

She texted to say she had to make a few house calls that night. She'd be home late. Would I pick up Maxito?

Of course.

The Chocolate Maven and Maxito and wildflowers and New Orleans.

I stopped at home to feed the chickens and grab everyone's dirty clothes to take to the laundromat. Picking up jeans and T-shirts and sweat pants and Spider-Man underwear, I screamed like a child when I saw the snake coiled on the tile floor at the foot of my bed. Beige and black, fat and archaic, I jumped back as the thing slithered away.

What was it?

"Did it have a pattern?" the guy who answered the phone at animal control wanted to know.

"Yes?"

"More like diamonds, or stripes?"

I didn't know. "It was fat and archaic," I whispered.

"It just darted away?"

"Yes." It had. Where was it now? Under the refrigerator?

"I wouldn't worry, ma'am," he said. "A rattler would've held its ground. Probably just a garter. It'll slither out the same way it came in."

I texted Abra: *Snake in the house. What does it mean?*

Surely a snake in the house was an omen.

She texted right back: *I guess it means we live in rural New Mexico?*

Yes. Maybe that's all it meant. We lived in rural New Mexico. Snakes needed a place to hide, too.

Abra texted again: *Probably because no one's been home for a few days.*

I texted right back: *Why hasn't anyone been home?*

But she didn't answer me.

Relax, Ariel. It'll slither out the same way it came in. I had errands to run. Laundry and the Chocolate Maven and Maxito and wildflowers and New Orleans.

I drove the 20 minutes into Santa Fe, read Dashiell Hammett at the laundromat.

When I pulled into the parking lot of the Chocolate Maven, I was thinking *Belgian chocolate torte or coconut cream cake?*

I scored a parking place right in front of the place, turned off the ignition.

The Chocolate Maven and Maxito and wildflowers and New Orleans. Yes. I could fix this. Café Du Monde in the French Quarter. All those Mardi Gras bands. It would be so romantic.

But when I pushed open the glass door to the café, I froze at the sight of them: Sitting across from each other at a little rectangular bistro table, Sol and Bipa, faces painted in full mime white and black, gloved hands open and moving together in synchronized pantomime.

Bipa moved one hand in a clockwise circular motion and

Sol followed. Bipa moved her other hand counterclockwise and Sol followed.

My body felt like it was shrinking in on itself. I stepped back. They hadn't seen me yet. I could still just recede into my humiliation.

But just then the hostess chirped, "Joining us for dinner?" and Sol and Bipa looked up, two startled mimes in their grease-white make-up and their black berets.

Bipa held up her gloved hands theatrically, like maybe this was a stick up.

Sol sat up straight. "Ariel!" she tried, as if they'd been waiting for me to join them and where was my makeup? Where was my beret?

I took another step back. Rewind everything and I'd be in my car again and on my way to pick up Maxito from preschool and I'd have changed my mind about cake and wildflowers and New Orleans and everything would go back to the normal silent irritation and resigned tolerance.

As I backed out of the place, I thought I heard Sol say, "Don't be dramatic, Ariel," but then the glass door was shut and I was in my car, engine on, and I was driving fast, gagging on pride.

I called in a pizza order. Half pepperoni with cheese and half green chile with spinach, no cheese.

I picked Maxito up from preschool.

"I'm great at puzzles," he announced as I buckled him into his car seat.

I WAS STILL shaking when we got home to our little adobe, didn't understand why I was shaking. *What was I so upset about?* Hadn't I just texted Vivian: *Jealous?*

"I love pizza with meat," Maxito beamed as I opened the box.

And the two of us sat on our big red couch, eating pizza and watching Joan Crawford in *Mildred Pierce* and laughing at the shadowy scenes and drinking sparkling water and pretty soon I wasn't shaking anymore and Maxito fell asleep in the crook of my arm and I carried him to bed and put a Lucinda Williams CD on in the living room and wished I had a beer and it wasn't too long before I heard the car tires in the driveway and the front door slam and Sol stomped in, still in full mime-face and wearing that black beret. She went right for boom box, pressed eject, put on Steely Dan. She turned to me, gloved hands on her hips. "What?" she demanded. "People aren't allowed to mime now?"

I sighed.

"You've always been jealous and paranoid," she said. "You embarrassed everyone, backing out of there like some pariah."

"Go to hell," I whispered, maybe too quiet.

"You know." Sol cleared her throat. "You didn't grow up with either of your parents loving you. Maybe you're just not capable of receiving love. Hmm?"

That unspeakable thing: If you've ever been mistreated, you're not worthy of care.

Steely Dan sang "Reeling in the Years" and "Rikki Don't Lose That Number." I'd never thought much either way about Steely Dan but now I felt with my whole body how much I hated Steely Dan, how much I had always hated Steely Dan. I thought, *Seriously? I'm Ariel Gore. I have 3,000 friends on Facebook and a closet full of really sexy boots. What am I doing with this miming jerk?*

Live with me for a year? Then you may ask questions?

I felt like I had gravel in my throat, but I opened my mouth anyway. I had a question. "Did we move to Santa Fe for that mime?" I wanted to know the answer. "Do Maxito and my dying mother and I all live in Santa Fe because we stalked a mime with you?"

Sol looked scared. Or maybe people in that white-and-black makeup always looked scared. Kind of startled and confused at the same time. "You think I'm stalking Bipa?" The flecks in her eyes weren't magic. They just looked mean. "Jesus, Ariel, you're just as crazy as *both* your parents."

Maybe I was, but not the kind of crazy she was talking about. I felt free and lonely. I wanted to run barefoot out the door and into the night, up the dirt road to Tex's place. I wanted to find him in his underground bunker and we'd drink Silver Coyote whiskey from a liter bottle and we'd yell at the moon about everyone who was out to get us. No, I had no problem with crazy right then.

Sol stared at me.

I knew I could still fix this if I wanted to. I could say: *Oh, I'm so sorry, I've been under so much stress and you're right I'm crazy and thank you for putting up with me all these years – I'm jealous and paranoid and of course people are allowed to mime* – and then I could lean into her warmth and she'd pat me on the back and kiss me on the head and say *Don't worry, it's all right.*

I thought about saying it. But then I remembered missing the 5:34 train and the girl in Albuquerque and those cold bricks on my back and now anything that started with *Oh, I'm so sorry* sounded like thanking someone for not kicking me in the ribs as I slept.

I'd promised not to do that.

So I just said, "Go to hell," louder this time, "and take the fucking Steely Dan with you."

Sol in her black and white face paint. She took her phone out of her pocket, texted somebody something, shook her head. "You're paranoid, Ariel."

I said, "And you're a mime stalker." Because I'm mature like that.

She said, "You're *completely* paranoid." But she didn't hold her ground. She stepped up to the boom box and pressed eject. She checked her phone. "Well," she said, finally taking off that beret. "Can I stay in the trailer for a couple of nights at least? Abra probably won't mind moving into the living room."

I shrugged. "Whatever."

Sol kind of bowed her head. "It's just that I can't move into Bipa's earthship until Tuesday."

And I had to laugh at that.

Just because you're paranoid doesn't mean your girlfriend's not stalking a mime.

I WANTED WINGS and tattoos, whiskey and the girl in Albuquerque. I craved so many things right then. But mostly I breathed relief. I needed to focus. All I had to do was keep my mouth shut for ten more minutes and I'd be free. *Don't say you're sorry. Ariel.*

I crawled into bed with my phone, left Sol and Abra to work out the sleeping arrangements. *Don't say you're sorry. Ariel.* By morning not even the Chocolate Maven and wild flowers and New Orleans could fix this. *Don't say you're sorry*. I didn't bother to change out of my jeans and sweatshirt, just wrapped my quilt around me, stared up at the vigas and the dark skylight. A place to mend.

I hoped the snake really had slithered out the way it came in.

The ruin of everything. But I felt something like happiness.

I texted Maia: *Broke up with Sol.*

She texted right back: *I know. She already updated her Facebook profile.* Then she texted again: *Can I say congratulations, Mama? I love you this much. (Picture my little kid arms open wide).*

And for the first time in a long time, I fell into easy undrunk sleep.

21.
You Can't Afford to Look Cheap

"NEVER SETTLE FOR ANYTHING BUT FIRST CLASS," GAMMIE told me as we sped down the Pacific Coast Highway in that 1970s Cadillac she called Big Red. She wore a red silk blouse and a red silk scarf and smelled like Coco Chanel.

I smiled and nodded and said, "Okay" because I loved my Gammie like a tomato.

"You're not common," she said. "You can't afford to look cheap."

And I smiled more and nodded more and I still loved my Gammie in a way that tasted raw and whole, but truth told, I just thought she was a classist bitch when she said shit like that.

I was a teenage squatter with a fading black eye, my boyfriend in jail, and I'd just come to visit for a week because the squat was cold without him and maybe I wanted to feel like a little girl again just visiting her Gammie off the Pacific Coast Highway and here all my Gammie could think to say was, "Never settle for anything but first class."

MORE THAN 20 years later, maybe I knew what she meant. About settling. About not being common. About the way she was a classist, sure, but she was more than that.

GAMMIE HAD BRIGHT Picasso posters on her walls, leopard-print sheets on her bed.

In her walk-in closet, Gammie had a giant mirror with

lights all around it, and she'd sit there applying makeup like she was some kind of a movie star. Or maybe a stripper.

She wore Max Factor foundation. Dior lipstick. She brushed her long gray hair, then tied it into a bun. She poured herself her morning vodka and sipped it slow, then headed out for an early lunch with the ladies.

I stayed home, sat there in front of Gammie's big movie-star mirror applying Max Factor foundation and Clinique concealer, trying to cover up the fading bruise of my common black eye.

22.
The Winged House

AFTER SOL LEFT, I WOKE TOO EARLY IN THE MORNINGS, drank black coffee on my porch alone, watched the sun rise muted orange over a dead vineyard.

I didn't want to talk to friends. It was hard enough explaining why I didn't live with my mother anymore. *Had she finally died?* Not exactly. *Was she healing?* Probably not.

I had no better language for talking about divorce beyond failure or a victim-fest. What could I say? *Was Sol having an affair?* Not exactly. *Had I done something wrong?* I didn't think so.

The few people I did talk to got a shrug and, "It was a long time coming."

How could I explain about the mime and Steely Dan? About not really knowing what kind of music I liked anymore? About the reasons we'd moved to New Mexico? About trusting a stranger in an alley more than I trusted this woman who might have been my wife had the good voters of Oregon not gotten together and amended their constitution to keep me from making that mistake?

How could I explain that everything seemed a part of the self-same ugliness: All the death urges, the legacies of abuse and conquest, the poisoned lakes and rivers, the waving knife in the night between a mother and her child, and all the lies I had to tell myself daily to make all this violence seem necessary and inevitable.

I felt more comfortable with people I hardly knew, with

Abra and her friends from the Native Arts College, with the queers who'd brought the summer rain, with the nervous single mom and a few of our other righteously paranoid neighbors.

I invited them over evenings to drink and eat and play new music for me so I could start to think about what I liked.

Mornings when Maxito was home with me, he wiggled out of bed, excited to check on his chickens and collect the eggs.

He adjusted the pirate scarf around his head. "I love my chickens."

He stayed with Sol three days a week now. He came home miming sometimes, but otherwise he seemed to adjust.

I hadn't lived without a partner since I was 30; hadn't lived without a kid at home since I was a teenager. Now I was nobody's daughter and half the time nobody's keeper. Some days I felt high with the limitlessness of it all. I could sleep until midmorning if I wanted to, or drive to Mexico. But most days with Maxito gone, I just had the mild panicked feeling that I'd misplaced him.

I TOOK AN old painting out from the back of a closet: A wooden house with feathered wings taking flight against a blood-red sky. I'd been dragging that painting around since my first apartment with Maia.

Her kindergarten school counselor cornered me in the hallway once, holding up a crayon drawing of a flying house. "This image," she warned me, "it can be a sign of wanting to run away." The counselor was my age – maybe 24 by then – with a freshly pierced eyebrow.

I nodded, wanted the counselor to know I took warning signs seriously. "It might also be a sign that Maia's had a painting of a winged house hanging over her mantle all her life."

The counselor laughed at that, kind of embarrassed. "Well, yes. I'm sorry. I just learned about the flying house last week. I'm in grad school at the Alternative University."

The painting sat crooked in its frame now, but I nailed a hook into the adobe wall and hung it up.

ABRA ATE HER diabetic-friendly omelet, glanced up at that painting. "Is that Baba Yaga's house?" She peered around the living room with new eyes. "Is *this* Baba Yaga's house?"

I didn't think about it, just said "yes." And then, "Wait. Does that make me Baba Yaga?" I didn't mind being the old witch.

But Abra laughed. "You're too young to be Baba Yaga. We will call you Lady Yaga."

IN THE FAIRY tale, Baba Yaga's house walks around on chicken legs, doesn't fly with feathered wings, but somehow it made sense. This was Baba Yaga's house out here on the road no one would drive if they didn't live here. Maybe we'd come here just like the lost young souls in the stories – like Vasilisa – come seeking some light other than death, come to serve the irrational, to sort the poppy seeds from the dirt, to gather strength, to figure out how to trust ourselves.

"Look," Abra pointed with her chin toward the living room window. The first snow of winter's return.

I looked up. "Beautiful."

23.
If My Lungs Were Wings

I DROVE OUT AN UNNUMBERED COUNTRY ROAD, SWERVED to avoid a rattlesnake, almost crashed my car into a cottonwood. I caught my breath and checked the rearview, realized the snake was already dead. *Focus, Ariel.*

I drove the 20 minutes into town, The Shins on the CD player, and I did the things I did in town – picked up my mail from the post office, picked up apples and green chile from the southside farmer's market, picked up Maxito from preschool.

Back home, he played with his Hot Wheels and said "look, Mama, look, Mama," and I looked and I absently checked my email. Coupons from Urban Outfitters and Country Outfitter, a warning about a full moon in Taurus from Leslie, recommended readings from Amazon.com, an overdue bill from my car insurance company, and this: A subjectless message from *evedebona @yahoo.com*.

My first thought was that my mother died and someone was using her email account to send me the news. It had been more than a year since the original death date she'd written on her calendar in red ink. It had been some ten months since I'd last seen her – staring at me through the screen of her bedroom window. I took a deep breath, like breath might prepare me, but when I clicked the email open, I knew she'd written it herself.

From: *evedebona@yahoo.com*
Subject:
Date: *November 2, 2011 9:56:47 AM MDT*
To: *arielgore@earthlink.net*

Hi Tiniest,

I wrote a poem and it's getting published. What do you think?

SANGRE DE CRISTO

I live alone now
in the long shadow
of these mountains.

Tumors
fill my lungs
and I am growing thin.

By day the dead
visit me and we talk,
sometimes for hours.

At night the puma
leaves his cold cave
to pace outside my door.

I dream that my lungs
are the wings of a great butterfly,
my spine its body.

On waking
I recall everyone
whom I have loved,

and my heart,
touched by the sacred one,
begins to burn.

I read the poem a couple of times, didn't know exactly what to make of it, what my mother was trying to communicate. Maybe she was just reaching out, writer to writer, the way strangers sometimes did if they'd read my work and wanted to share their own. Maybe it was more than that. To reply felt like a risk, but I took it.

From: *arielgore@earthlink.net*
Subject: *Re:*
Date: *November 2, 2011 2:37:11 PM MDT*
To: *evedebona@yahoo.com*

Hi Mom,

Your poem is good.

Are you just sharing or would you like me to come and see you?

Ariel

From: *evedebona@yahoo.com*
Subject: *Re:*
Date: *November 2, 2011 2:41:16 PM MDT*
To: *arielgore@earthlink.net*

Hi Tiniest,

Sweet of you to write back. I hear you left Sol and moved back to Portland? Care to fill me in?

If you're in Santa Fe you could come by the house. I would like that. I have an appointment tomorrow, but I'll be back by noon.

Will you bring Maxito?

From: *arielgore@earthlink.net*
Subject: *Re:*
Date: *November 2, 2011 3:58:49 PM MDT*
To: *evedebona@yahoo.com*

I think I'll come alone.

Between noon and one?

From: *evedebona@yahoo.com*
Subject: *Re:*
Date: *November 2, 2011 4:00:07 PM MDT*
To: *arielgore@earthlink.net*

Wonderful.

"LOOK, MAMA!" MAXITO squealed. He let go of an orange Hot Wheels car and laughed as it loop-de-looped around the plastic track. "I love my Hot Wheels," he sighed. "Should we go see if my chickens made eggs?"

"Of course."

We barreled outside and around the house. Four chickens huddled together under their heat lamp, one balled up on the ground just outside the coop, but still inside the chicken-wire and bamboo fence.

Maxito's face fell. "Is Ping hurt?"

"Don't touch her, baby," I said, and I pulled on a pair of gardening gloves as I went to touch her.

Maxito's lip quivered as he watched.

"I don't know what happened," I told him. "Ping died." It wasn't particularly cold out. No blood or misplaced feathers evidenced attack.

We dug a grave for the chicken.

"Why did Ping die, Mama?'

"I don't know," I admitted. "Maybe she was sick."

Maxito wrinkled his nose. "That's sad."

MAXITO FELL ASLEEP early. Sol had come when I wasn't home and taken the bed we'd shared for ten years, so I curled up on the cowboy bedroll I'd patched together from cushions and blankets and I closed my eyes.

I dreamed I took a train to my mother's old house in southern Mexico, but when I got there she had this thick file of medical bills all in my name and said I had to pay them. She was showing me the bills, paging through them, thousands of dollars worth of alternative cancer treatments and old Kaiser X-rays. She was licking her index finger – those red manicured nails. "I know you don't have any money," she was saying, all calm and matter-of-fact. "I'm going to help you," she said. "You'll just have to sell me your liver and we'll be even."

I was screaming, horrified, "You can't just put bills in other people's names! You can't demand to buy somebody's liver!"

My mother shook her head. "I can see you're hysterical, Ariel."

I was running through white hallways, trying to get away. Some medical facility and all the doors chained shut. I was in a plastic body bag, ripping my way out. I was back in the kitchen in the house in Mexico. Dark now and my mother approached me. "Tiniest?" she whispered, and she reached to touch my face. I softened, surprised by her tenderness, but then she grabbed my throat to strangle me.

I woke coughing on my little cowboy bedroll on the floor, got up to check on Maxito, to watch the rise and fall of his chest. It was only midnight. I made myself a cup of chamomile tea.

Relax, Ariel. But then I thought of all the people who'd ever told me to relax and the way they were always the people who I shouldn't have relaxed around, should've done the opposite. Like the people who say "trust me." Nobody you should trust ever says, "trust me." Adrenaline up and run.

But I didn't run.

ONE P.M. THE next day and I pulled into the gravel driveway of the former duplex, parked next to my mother's new white Prius.

The sound of my boots in that gravel, familiar and faraway.

I approached the door, knocked, then knocked again. I tried the handle, but it was locked. If she'd blown her brains out in there and wanted me to find her, I reasoned, she probably would have left the door open.

She just wasn't home.

I left six eggs in a basket on her doormat, walked back to my car feeling like a chump.

What was I thinking, coming here?

I hated the part of myself that seemed to have this inextinguishable hope, but I didn't know how to snuff it out. I'd been reading my Buddhist books. Pema Chödrön said that, "Only to the extent that we expose ourselves over and over to annihilation can that which is indestructible in us be found." But I didn't want this naïve hope to be my indestructible part.

I wanted to be cooler than that.

I wanted to know better.

A deer sauntered down the dirt road in front of the former duplex. Our eyes locked for a second, but I shook my head. This place was just so over-the-top, like some dark and corny spaghetti Western come to life. The deer kept walking, slow and elegant.

I got in my car and turned my key, drove away in the long shadow of those mountains.

24.
The Mine Shaft Tavern

I DIDN'T HEAR FROM MY MOTHER THAT DAY OR THE NEXT. I made hot and sour soup with tofu and shiitake mushrooms, settled back into the idea that I might not see her again, that after a week or a year someone would notice the smell of death and I'd get the call I didn't know how to prepare for. The waiting manifested in a constant, low-level stabbing pain in my right shoulder, made me feel at once jaded and on edge, but I figured that not seeing her again would be all right.

Sure, some part of me would always be that magical-thinking four-year-old waiting for my good mother to rescue me from this witch, but I hadn't come all this way looking for my good mother. The only thing I'd written on my wrist all those months ago in Portland was *Behave in a way you're going to be proud of.*

I was sitting at my desk, futzing with a story on my computer and clicking around Pandora.com looking for music I might like when the email came through. The subject line alone filled me with sudden dread.

> **From:** *evedebona@yahoo.com*
> **Subject:** *Thanksgiving*
> **Date:** *November 13, 2011 4:01:06 AM MDT*
> **To:** *arielgore@earthlink.net*
>
> Dear Ariel,
>
> I am very aware that I missed our appointment the other day. The fresh eggs were delicious. Can we talk about Thanksgiving now? I

think it would be a good idea for you and Maia and Maxito to come here for the feast.

Love,

Mom

I IMAGINED PULLING into my mother's gravel driveway, my kids all dressed up, finding the place locked.

I envisioned the door open, the smell of roasting turkey and sweet potatoes, my mother wielding a giant carving knife with a handle made of bone.

I remembered the Thanksgivings of my childhood. My stepdad always kept a firm grip on the white bone of that carving knife.

I thought about refusing her invitation, inviting her to my little adobe south of town instead. But who's to say I wouldn't open the door, expecting to see my mother, and get a process server instead, legal papers in hand?

From: *arielgore@earthlink.net*
Subject: *Re: Thanksgiving*
Date: *November 13, 2011 8:02:34 AM MDT*
To: *evedebona@yahoo.com*

Hi Mom,

The kids and I would be happy to spend Thanksgiving with you, but we already have a plan. There's a bar out on Highway 14 called the Mine Shaft Tavern. It's in Madrid. Maybe 15 miles out past the penitentiary. They do a community Thanksgiving. You're welcome to join us.

Ariel

From: *evedebona@yahoo.com*
Subject: *Re: Thanksgiving*
Date: *November 13, 2011 8:03:21 AM MDT*
To: *arielgore@earthlink.net*

At a bar?!?

YES. THE MINE Shaft Tavern. It seemed the appropriate place to emerge from underground.

My mother didn't RSVP to my Thanksgiving bar invitation, but it was all I had to offer. I didn't want to bring my kids to her house and I didn't want to give her my address. I would behave in a way I was going to be proud of, and she could take it or leave it. Maia and Maxito and I would spend the day together regardless. Abra and her one white friend from the Native Arts College would meet us there, too. Sol would come pick Maxito up later in the evening for a second dinner at her place.

So it was Thanksgiving afternoon and we set out from our little adobe, took the back roads into the Ortiz Mountain range, headed south and west on that winding desert highway into the glare of the November sun.

Maia wore a tight black dress with a fur collar, stiletto heels. She pushed a Black Keys CD into the player.

"Do you think Nonna will show up?" I asked her.

"Oh, she'll show up," Maia hummed.

"Who's Nonna?" Maxito asked form the back seat.

I looked at him in the rearview.

He tugged at his clip-on bow tie.

"She's your grandmother, honey. Maybe you'll remember her when you see her."

We rolled into Madrid, that Old West town half a parody of itself. The Mine Shaft's parking lot full of hogs and trucks and VW vans. The bar spilled over with bikers and cowboys and hippies. All leather jackets and cowboy boots and the smell of flowers and patchouli. I recognized the white girl with dreadlocks who'd come into the candle shop to warn me that Sol was leaving notes for Bipa at the mime school. My skittish single mom neighbor huddled with her kids at a table near the fireplace, avoided eye contact with anyone.

We grabbed a long wooden table in the corner.

No band played, so a dozen preschoolers had taken over the raised back corner of the bar, squealing as they stage-dived.

Maxito sidled up to join them, stood shy on the periphery at first, then jumped in and lead the gang until he limped back to the table, flushed and worn-out.

We didn't have to wonder after my mother for long.

"Nonna!" Maia yelled.

Gray dress and red lipstick. She floated in on the arm of a six-foot-five black man who she introduced first to the bartender and then to all of us as "my son the surgeon" despite their obvious lack of physical resemblance.

"No Ronaldo?" Maia mouthed.

My mother rolled her eyes. "I suppose he's with his wife." She looked me up and down. "Happy Thanksgiving. Have you lost weight?"

Maxito kept his eyes on his grandmother as she moved back and forth through the crowd.

The cowboys in their tight jeans and turquoise belt buckles glanced up at her from their seats at the bar when she passed. She flirted and danced with them, Dixie Chicks and Rascal Flatts singing through the speakers, wood floorboards creaking. My mother laughed.

THE SURGEON NUDGED me as we waited in the potluck line for turkey and greens. "I hope you know she's leaving *everything* to me."

I picked up a dinner roll, spread it with Earth Balance, nudged him back and winked. "I hope you know there isn't anything to leave."

The surgeon frowned as he piled his plate with mashed potatoes, poured the vegan gravy.

I hadn't had a drink since Sol left – sought the clarity of sobriety – but I was ready for a beer. I set my plate on the bar and ordered a pint of Dead Canary Ale.

Maia had finally turned 21, but nobody asked her for an ID when she shouldered up next to me and asked for a Bloody Mary.

"HOW DO YOU like the Native Arts College?" the surgeon asked Abra's friend at the long table.

The girl shook her blonde locks. "The Native people are very racist against whites."

"I can imagine," the surgeon scratched his chin, like he took her seriously. "Those racist Native Americans. That's been going on for hundreds of years."

Abra laughed at that, but the blonde girl nodded like she'd finally found someone who understood her pain.

Maia smirked as she cut into her smoked turkey. "This might be more similar to the original Thanksgiving than anything I've ever experienced."

Family and strangers sharing a meal; toothy smiles as if we weren't all in it for the kill.

A PAUL SIMON song started through the speakers and my mother glided back to our table. "I love this place," she sighed, and she put her arm around the surgeon. "You're such a dear man to bring your mother here for her *last* Thanksgiving."

Maxito stared at her, then glanced at Maia, at the surgeon, at Abra and at Abra's friend, and then at me, his four-year-old heart/mind taking it all in. "I like turkey," he said softly as he stuck his fork into the pile of meat on his paper plate. "I just really like turkey."

Maia lifted her Bloody Mary and shrugged. "Let's not even list what we're thankful for this year."

Book Four

The Feasts of Baba Yaga

25.
Marked Women

"OH, DARLING," THE VOICE THAT ANSWERED MY MOTHER'S landline had a British accent. "I've just rung the ambulance."

Cold January morning and I sat sipping black coffee on the porch of my little adobe. "Ambulance?"

"Yes, darling. I'm your Mum's palliative care nurse. We're just taking her to the hospital to get her pain under control."

Palliative care nurse. I scooted the words around in my brain. "From hospice?"

"No, darling," the voice said. "Your Mum got herself booted from hospice again."

I pulled a blanket around my shoulders, stared at the round-top mountain I could see from my porch. I was alone in the house for now – Maxito off with Sol for a few days, Maia back in Los Angeles, Abra not yet home from winter break.

I'D SPENT DECEMBER house sitting for a friend in Portland. Took Maia and Maxito to the *Nutcracker* ballet.

Hot Wheels and Lego sets and a tattoo gift certificate under the tree.

At Oddball Studios off Clinton Street, Maia got a portrait of Gammie as a 1940s pin-up. "Your great grandmother was a pin-up?" The tattoo artist with an anchor inked on his neck seemed impressed when Maia unfurled the old picture from *The Los Angeles Times*. Gammie sitting arched-back on the sand in her bathing suit, coy smile up to the camera, with the caption "Beauty on the Beach."

I'd emailed back and forth with my mother a few times from Portland, told her I could help her out on Wednesdays when I got back to New Mexico. I figured I could handle Wednesdays. One day a week. And the first Wednesday had gone well enough. When I got there she was screaming at some worker in the entryway and he scurried off with his hammer muttering, "your mother's a witch."

But my mother shook her head. "That guy had ego problems."

I gave her a quick hug and she flinched when I touched her shoulder.

She wore a loose black sweater, pointed to the lightbulbs in the kitchen that needed changing.

The kitchen. A six-burner commercial gas stove, rustic faux-finished cabinets, antiqued metal and mahogany counters, a deep farmhouse sink. When I stood on the stepladder I didn't worry that she might push me. She seemed too weak for that kind of thing now.

I took her shopping list to Healthy Wealthy, bought organic chanterelle mushrooms and mint citrus tea.

When I got back, she asked about Maxito, said, "All right, thanks, Tiniest. I'll see you next week."

NOW IT WAS Wednesday again and I held the phone to my cold ear.

"Don't worry, darling," the voice said. "We'll get your mum settled in and you can come along and meet us at the hospital later this afternoon."

"I can come now," I offered. It wasn't that I felt any pressing need to rush to my mother's bedside, it was that I had a date with a cute chef I'd been flirting with on Facebook and I didn't want to get held up at the hospital. I mean, I'd gotten my legs waxed. That's what I was thinking: *I just got my legs waxed.*

"No, darling," the palliative care nurse said. "You'll meet us at Christus Saint Vincent's Hospital later this afternoon."

I thought to argue, but the voice sounded like somebody's good mother, so I said, "All right," and I hung up thinking, *Please, God, my mother's already ruined my life. Don't let her wreck my date.*

The cute chef on Facebook was a friend of a friend. She'd just buried her father, said she only wanted red chile and new tattoos. I'd told her I agreed that death and chile and tattoos were an excellent combination, but I didn't tell her I knew anything about dying parents.

I messaged her from my cold porch now: *Collecting new reasons to get tattooed by the minute.* I wanted stars on my hips.

She didn't ask for further explanation and I didn't offer any. She just messaged back: *Still on for 5 o'clock, I hope?*

I hoped so, too.

INSIDE, I TOOK a random book from the shelf. *In Quest of Candlelighters* by Kenneth Patchen. I ran my hand across the black and white cover, asked: *What now?* I opened to a random page and read this: "My God I can smell death all around me." I shook my head, wanted to shake it off. *What kind of an oracle was that?* I wanted to try again, turned the page and read instead, "right now I insist that right now some beautiful girl is sitting on the bank of a river with a copy of this book in her hands and right now she has a rose in her hair."

Yes. This could be my new oracle.

There would be an end to all this death someday. Fast forward and *right now some beautiful girl is sitting on the bank of a river with a copy of this book and right now she has a rose in her hair.*

I PULLED INTO the parking lot of the hospital on the hill at 3:30 that afternoon. The buildings were adobe-brown like all the buildings in Santa Fe.

The sound of my boots on asphalt, automatic sliding glass door, boots on tile.

Inside, all white walls and low ceilings, paintings of desert rocks and Native women. Santa Fe paintings.

The man who sat behind glass wrote my mother's room number on a card for me. Lay people with "volunteer" badges pinned to their chests shuffled through the hallways carrying clipboards and offering communion to some of the patients.

An old man in a baseball hat gave me a brochure with the word "healing" above a crucifix.

I thanked him, stepped into the elevator, opened the brochure. *Good news! Jesus has already borne your sickness, so you don't have to!*

A right turn down the hall, then right again. I didn't think much of it all. I'd been to see my mother in plenty of hospital rooms back in Portland. But when I peered around the doorframe into her room, the sight of her made my breath catch.

She sat propped in a chair, her eyes closed, head back and mouth open. Surrounded by machines that beeped and glowed. An oxygen tube in her nose.

I stepped back from the doorway to steady my breath. What had I expected, anyway? The mother of my childhood? Dark 1970s perm? Defined biceps, still strong enough to leave a mark when she hit me?

I crept into the room, quiet as I could, but she opened her eyes right away and smiled. "Tiniest?"

I set the healing brochure on her bedside table. "You better be careful," I warned her. "There's a whole lot of Jesus up in this place."

She laughed, kind of shrugged but then didn't shrug–winced at the shrugging. "I got no problem with Jesus," she said. She had black radiation tattoos inked across her chest. There was the alternate beeping of the heart monitor and the morphine pump. The sound of the oxygen machine. "Ariel?" she said suddenly. "You look gorgeous."

I gestured toward her morphine pump. "I bet everybody looks pretty good when you're on all those drugs."

She smiled, but tears welled in her eyes. "Tiniest?" She sighed. "You came back to me."

I sat down on a cushioned pink chair in the corner of the room, scooted closer to her. "I only came because I heard you were going to be on your best behavior from now on."

She wrinkled her nose. "I must have been on a *lot* of drugs if I told anyone *that*."

And I had to laugh.

I knew my mother was impossible, and worse. But some part of me had always liked her.

NURSES AND ATTENDANTS shuffled in and out of the room, adjusted the machines and brought white bread sandwiches and plastic cups of red Jello.

My mother scowled at the trays. "Can you imagine serving this to someone in a *hospital?* Give me a piece of paper. I have a shopping list for you."

I kept my eye on the wall clock as she wrote her list in red ink. "I have to go in a few minutes," I told her. "I can bring you the food tomorrow."

"Go?" She looked panicked, wrote faster.

"I have to pick up Maxito," I lied.

Tears rushed down her cheeks. "I need a book, Tiniest. You can't leave me here without a book. *Please*. I need you to go to the bookstore for me."

Florescent light and the smell of disinfectant.

"I can't, Mom."

Her face crumpled. "I'm begging you, Tiniest. I'll die of boredom in this place. They'll turn on the *television* and it won't be Anderson Cooper. It will be some idiotic thing. Some ... reality cops."

I could feel my heart contract in my chest, but *no. I was going on a date. I wasn't going to the bookstore*. Maybe my date would be hot and easy or maybe it would be strained and awkward – I didn't care – my mother was not going to be the one to ruin it for me. "I'll go and see if I have anything in my car," I offered. My car was a disaster heap of Christmas cards and overdue bills and clothes and toys. Surely there would be a book in there somewhere.

Tile hall, elevator, tile steps, glass doors, asphalt.

Nothing in the back seat.

I dug through the trunk, finally found a hardback some publishing company had sent as a review copy a long time ago. *Free From Lies*. I squinted at the subtitle, *Discovering Your True Needs*. Who knew what it was about?

My mother was asleep when I stepped back into her room, so I left the book on her bedside table and pocketed her red-ink shopping list.

THE CHEF TEXTED directions to her house. She lived on a busy street, driveway exposed, so I parked around the corner. I didn't need anyone in this small town whispering about where they'd seen my car. I carried a basket of fresh eggs down the block and up the walkway to her door.

The chef. She was cuter than her profile picture, had a shy swagger, gray hair and blue eyes. She invited me in, offered me a glass of wine.

I thought her house seemed too clean, but I wrote it off to the recent death.

We wore the same black engineer boots, sat on her leather couch.

IN MY MEMORY, I told the chef about my mother.

In her memory, I did not.

I'D BEEN READING about the "cognitive deficits" caused by stress and grief. That the two of us could carry on a conversation is, apparently, impressive. The fact that neither of us would later remember what we'd said is, it turns out, perfectly normal.

I REMEMBER SHE showed me the African violets she'd had inked on her upper arm the day after her father's funeral. Just the black outlines and gray shading so far. The skin around it had just started to peel. She said she liked the physical and tangible pain of that. Death and tattoos.

But when we stepped into the studio on Topeka Street maybe an hour later, all the artists were booked up.

It would just be a red chile night.

Enchiladas at the mall.

I remember a table by the window.

I remember I touched the chef's arm.

I remember comparing exes to make sure we had at least three degrees of separation.

I remember that I laughed.

NEXT MORNING I woke alone on my cowboy bedroll in my little adobe, wasn't so cold.

I'd agreed to meet the chef back at the tattoo shop just before noon. We arrived wearing the same brown Frye harness boots and she blushed at that, watched over a low wall as a boy with a butterfly on his face etched stars into my skin. Each black outline and each gold shading hurt in just the right ways, deep and hungry. I wanted to scar myself like this with talismans. I wanted to ward off all the hard things that hadn't happened yet. I wanted to remember these cold days; remember how it felt to be cut like this, to ache and to bruise, to peel and tend the wound, to heal.

26.
What We All Call Love

ASPHALT, GLASS DOORS, TILE STEPS, ELEVATOR, TILE hall.

"Tiniest," my mother cried from the crisp white sheets of her hospital bed. She held up the hard cover review copy of *Free from Lies*. "*Why* did you have this book in your car? I will *pay* for the therapy. I will *go* to the therapy with you. If you were abused like this, I'll do *anything*."

My face must have flushed. I looked down at my brown harness boots. "I haven't read that book," I admitted. "It was ... a review copy. What is it?"

"Oh God," my mother sighed. Her tattooed eyeliner looked strange now that she didn't wear any other makeup. "Oh, thank *God*. Tiniest, this book is heaven-sent. It's the single most important book ever written. It's by Alice Miller. *I* was abused, Tiniest." She lifted her hand weakly, pointed to her chest. "Do you know that? *I* was abused. I'm so glad you weren't abused."

I set down the grocery bag from Healthy Wealthy. Didn't clarify that I'd only said I hadn't read the book.

"This is why I have cancer," my mother cried. "I have lung cancer because I was abused and I didn't have enough time to get free."

I sat down in the pink-cushioned chair by her bed. "I'm sorry."

THOSE FIRST DAYS in the hospital my mother wept easily.

In the mornings I brought her organic quinoa salad and senna tea.

She complimented me on my good looks, read passages aloud from the pages of *Free From Lies*. She liked the chapter that began with a scene from "Mommie Dearest." Christina Crawford at her mother's deathbed, tears in her eyes. "I've always loved you," the daughter said. "You've suffered so much, but now you are freed of those sufferings."

I tried not to laugh, thinking about the wire hanger scene and my mother in her facemask reenacting it when I was a kid. But I knew she didn't think it was funny now.

She read Alice Miller's analysis: "This scene pinpoints the tragedy of abused children. Their own sufferings count for nothing."

My fresh tattoos still stung.

The hissing sound of my mother's oxygen machine.

"*My* suffering," my mother cried, "it counted for *nothing*, Tiniest." She steadied herself, kept reading about the abused children: "They have so completely internalized the determination of the parents and society to ignore what they have been through that they can only feel compassion for their parents, never for the children they themselves were. This is what we all call love." My mother flinched, pressed the button on her morphine pump. "Waiting for love is not love," she whispered, the book shaking in her hand now. "Waiting for love is not love, even if we always call it that." One of her machines started beeping and she squinted at me. "Do you understand, Ariel?"

I didn't say anything. Of course I understood. My heart ached for the child my mother once was. But my compassion had these bruised and angry edges. I thought, *seriously? You have the nerve to complain to me?* Part of me just wanted to rip all the tubes out of her body and watch her die in slow agony.

"Yes," I finally said. "I understand."

AFTERNOONS UNDER THOSE fluorescent lights, we met with oncologists and social workers.

My mother had finally agreed to Western medical treatment because one doctor promised he could relieve her pain by shrinking the tumor at the back of her neck with radiation, but now another doctor admitted that the tumor had been the only thing holding her spine up. Her thoracic vertebrae had collapsed. She'd need more morphine.

"I have a lot of work to do," she whispered. "I just need to get back to where I was at Thanksgiving. I can get better, can't I?"

The oncologist stood at the foot of her bed, nodding. "Yes, perhaps."

But when I approached him in the hallway later and said, "talk to me," he closed the file he held, cleared his throat, adjusted his glasses. "Your mother's cancer is unusually slow-growing," he said softly. "At this rate she could easily live for five more years. But with metastases to the spine – the worst-case scenario?"

I looked down at my boots, then back at him. "Hit me."

"One vertebrae collapses at a time. You're looking at complete paralysis within six months. She'll need round-the-clock care at home and obviously you need to talk to her social worker, but off the record I don't think Medicare will cover it." He motioned with his chin to someone and the social worker appeared as if she'd been waiting for the cue.

She stuck out her hand. "I'm Melissa," she chirped. She wore a purple angora sweater. "Your mother might be eligible for Casa Que Pasa. It's a ... facility. There's certainly no guarantee she'd be eligible, with Medicare and in her condition it's unlikely, but we can get started on the paperwork?"

"I don't know." If the exposé I'd read about Casa Que Pasa in the local weekly newspaper could be believed, even Joan Crawford didn't deserve to end up there. The patients sat around in dirty adult diapers as lawsuits alleging negligence piled up. Patients who'd fallen, breaking legs or femurs, were just put back in bed – no X-rays and no treatment. The health department had cited the place for improperly administering medication and for failing to protect residents from abuse. The article went on and on. Casa Que Pasa was maybe the worst in New Mexico and New Mexico was maybe the worst in the country and, no, I shook my head, "My mother isn't going to Casa Que Pasa."

I crept back into her room, sat next to her until she opened her eyes. "What do you want to have happen? When they release you?"

She shook her head. "They can't release me."

Her new roommate wretched and coughed alone on the other side of the curtain, cried, "you eat it" to no one I could see.

My mother grimaced in the curtain's direction.

"Technically, you're just here to finish this round of radiation," I tried to explain. "And they actually want to stop the radiation. Eventually they'll release you. I need to know if you've thought about what you want."

My mother didn't answer me. She closed her eyes. "Nothing is secret," she whispered. "Nothing is secret anymore, Tiniest."

EVENINGS WHEN MAXITO was with Sol, the chef texted me the names of unfamiliar restaurants. We showed up in the same Doc Martens we'd dug out from the backs of our closets. She started adding to the end of her texts: *Which boots are you wearing?*

I ordered breakfast at night.

In a booth at Tortilla Flats, she leaned across the table, and offered to kill my mother. "You know," she said, "if it comes to that."

I knew I liked her then.

My friends on Facebook were "sending love and light," but I needed a darker kind of tenderness.

We made out in the parking lot under the stars and the neon lights. Her skin.

"I like this part," I whispered.

"Which part?"

The part when we weren't yet lovers, but we might be. The part when I dreamed of her voice. The part before the hurt set in.

ASPHALT, GLASS DOORS, tile steps, elevator, tile hall.

Two weeks in the hospital and my mother didn't cry so easily anymore. She just seemed high. She grabbed at my hands. "Your rings are sparkly," she said, "tell me about your day, Tiniest. Tell me everything."

I didn't want to tell her about the chef, didn't want to admit I didn't have Maxito full time, didn't want to give her anything she could use against me when she made some miraculous recovery. Instead, I showed her Facebook pictures of Leslie with her new boyfriend in Portland.

"He looks like a wonderful man," my mother sighed, then shook her head, winced at the pain of shaking her head.

When the woman wearing the Jesus T-shirt came in, offering the roommate behind the curtain communion, my mother protested. "I want communion."

The woman startled. "I'm sorry dear. I didn't have you listed as Catholic." Still, she approached my mother's bedside, placed the wafer on my mother's tongue and began, "Lord, I am not worthy ... "

My mother bit down fast. "I *am* worthy," she spat. "I totally deserve this wafer."

The woman in the Jesus T-Shirt stepped back, wide-eyed, sputtered something about a healing soul as she backed out of the room.

My mother shook her head, shook it slowly so as not to hurt herself. "I mean, could they at least *try* to make you feel good? Can you guess what they gave me for dinner last night? What was in between the two slices of Wonder bread? In a *hospital?*"

"Processed meat?"

"Yes, processed meat. In a *hospital*. And then they say I'm not worthy?"

"It's just a Catholic thing, Mom, the traditional Catholics – they say that to everyone."

But she kept shaking her head. "Processed meat. In a *hospital*."

MAXITO AND I cruised through the aisles of Healthy Wealthy. He'd learned to decipher food labels, knew he was only allowed ten grams of sugar at a sitting. He pointed right and then left, granola bars and cheddar cheese, bread and lettuce.

I bought butternut squash and gluten-free macaroni. Abra was back now and the kids from the Native Arts College piled into our little adobe south of town for Thursday night dinners. Maxito made himself lettuce sandwiches and enticed the guests to jump with him on his trampoline.

Carter Quark, the trans guy everyone said I should date after Sol left, brought beer. I thought he was too young for me, but he made me laugh and seemed to know everyone. He already knew Abra anyway, and he already knew the chef. Carter Quark. He was just one of those guys people called by both first and last names.

"I'm trying to seduce the chef," I confided.

His eyes brightened at that. "Glorious. I've *been* there, but I'm sure you'll make more progress than I did."

I laughed. "You think?"

"I do." Carter adjusted his bow tie, sipped his beer. "Let me know if there's *anything* I can do to help."

ASPHALT, GLASS DOORS, tile steps, elevator, tile hall.

I watched from the doorway of my mother's room. She had a new visitor, a strange blonde woman with a German accent who talked and cried under the fluorescent lights as my mother drifted in and out.

She had a full necklace now, my mother – those radiation tattoos.

Her strange friend stood like a preacher, read to her from

a new age book about finding one's soulmate. "Come on," my mother's friend insisted. "Don't you want a new lover, Eve?"

My mother laughed, adjusted her oxygen tube, closed her eyes.

I left them there. Tile hall, elevator, tile steps, glass doors, asphalt.

NEW LOVER. I flicked the words under my tongue. *My new lover.* The chef made me think of shark teeth and orchids. She was lovely like jagged rocks along the shore. I followed her home.

She said, "Come around to the kitchen door. Can we be discreet?" She made me hot red chile sauce, poured it over homemade tortillas, whispered, "This. Try this."

On the edge of her couch, she rubbed lotion into my healing star tattoos.

She pulled me into her bedroom, whispered, "Is this all right?" She held my uneven ribs, licked the salt from my skin, whispered, "May I fuck you?"

I slept, fist balled on her chest. Woke legs entwined, like I'd slept there with her a thousand nights. And in the icy light through the window above her bed, I thought maybe I was learning how to stand firm where there is no ground. Learning how to hold this sadness.

Three weeks.

My legs were still smooth.

HOT WATER ON the stove in the chef's little kitchen and my phone buzzed too early.

"Oh, darling." It was the British accent. The palliative care nurse I'd never met. "I've just learned they're releasing your Mum from the hospital later today."

I stared out the chef's window. The bare branches of winter trees.

"They're releasing her to you, darling."

I didn't say anything. Just watched the trees against the

morning sky. My mother couldn't get herself to the bathroom now, couldn't eat solid food, needed the oxygen tank to breathe.

"Hospice will deliver a hospital bed to the house, darling, and we'll get her pain stabilized on the fentanyl patch and the morphine pump. We've got her accepted into a new hospice service and the nurses will come along and check on her every day."

"I can't take care of her," I squeaked.

But the voice just said, "I know, darling. I know."

27.
Pirates are Beautiful

THE COLD BRIGHT OF THE DAY HELD STEADY.

Delivery men wearing dark blue T-shirts showed up at the former duplex to install the hospital bed in my mother's room.

Nurses with name tags brought bedpans and enemas and walkers and machines with battery packs.

A man in light blue scrubs asked me to sign for the oxygen machine. He showed me how to use it so quickly that when he left I just sat down on the Saltillo tile floor and cried.

Sol called about something, said, "You sound like hell, Ariel. What's wrong with you?"

And I thanked God that I didn't have to do any of this to a Steely Dan soundtrack. I clicked the phone off, put Etta James on instead.

Runners from a pharmacy in Albuquerque came to the door with lunch bags full of prescription medications. Now we had morphine and fentanyl and Ativan and Oxycodone and Haldol and a dozen other pills and patches for pain and nausea and psychosis.

The palliative care nurse I'd only talked to on the phone appeared at the open door, walked in without knocking, red hair and turquoise cowboy boots. Tired gray eyes. She smiled and I never wanted her to leave me. "Are you managing, darling?" She cooed.

What could I say? I was trying very hard to manage.

"The night nurses cost twenty dollars an hour, darling,"

she said. She sat down at the dining room table, started writing things on a half sheet of paper. Here was the number for the night nurses. Another service in town might send nursing students for ten dollars an hour, she said, but we had to go through an intake process. Here was that number. We'd need baby monitors so we could hear my mother from anywhere in the house. We'd need adult diapers, sippy cups, baby wipes, disinfecting wipes, soothing music, receiving blankets, soft foods.

I remembered a dream I'd had back in Portland when my mother was first diagnosed. A dream I was unexpectedly pregnant, crossing a desert border panicked and confused. I woke thinking that wasn't a normal dream for a lesbian – unexpected pregnancy – but it all made more sense now.

I left the palliative care nurse in the house, ducked out to buy the baby products. It occurred to me that someone should throw me a "hospice shower." Maybe I could register at "Dying Parents 'R' Us," make a big tres leches cake. Then it occurred to me that I was perhaps getting a little bit morbid in my middle age.

I called the night nurse service from a parking lot. *Yes, I needed someone for the first three nights at least.* I did the math. All these nurse hours would add up, but there was no way I could move into the former duplex full-time again. My mother's social security check would pay for ten nurse-nights a month. It boggled my mind to think that people poorer than me dealt with this kind of thing every day. People with less flexible jobs. I stopped at the new candle shop that had replaced ours, bought a Virgin of Guadalupe, headed to the Southside to pick up Maxito from his Spanish immersion daycare.

I knocked on the arched door the way I always knocked.

Maxito's pretty teacher opened the door the way she always opened it, but she didn't quite make eye contact. Two unfamiliar white people stood behind her.

I could see Maxito and his friend Diego playing with colored blocks in the main room, but something was off. The place smelled skunky like weed and smoke. "Everything all right?"

"Not really," Maxito's teacher hummed.

One of the white people piped up. "We're with the Children, Youth and Families Department. We've suspended Ms. Martinez' license until she works out a number of issues. This day care facility is now closed."

Ms. Martinez' lip quivered, but I just shook my head. Of course this day care facility was now closed.

I took Maxito's little sweaty hand in mine, led him outside. As I lifted him into his car seat, he bit his lip. "Will I be able to play with Diego tomorrow?"

I squinted into the afternoon sun, buckled him in. "Probably not tomorrow. But you'll see him again soon. How about we go get a Lego set?"

"A pirate set?"

"Sure."

Subject: *We need help in Santa Fe*
From: *arielgore@earthlink.net*
Date: *January 31, 2012 4:57:20 PM MST*
To: *<undisclosed recipients>*

Greetings friends and friends of Eve,

As many of you know, my mom was diagnosed with Stage IV lung cancer over two years ago. Her health has taken a sudden turn, and I need your help now.

After three weeks in the hospital, she's being released into home hospice care. This is not a 24-7 care service. I need friends willing to come for a few days or week each to help her here at home.

Please let me know if you can take on any time in February or March.

Thanks so much,

Ariel

I SENT THE email to the twenty or so old friends I could think of. No one I knew of had come to visit since we'd moved to New

Mexico, but maybe now they would come. I hated to sound helpless, had been trained that asking for help meant I was a loser, but I had to grow up. I had to admit there was no way I could pull this off by myself.

Like a miracle they wrote back. A few of them wrote back, anyway. Yes, maybe they could come. They would check their calendars. Yes, three days or a week? They could probably commit to that. They'd had their hard times with Eve, they said, but they loved her. Maybe they even had some frequent flyer miles. They would check.

Leslie would come for a week if I bought her a ticket. Her son, Leo, would come next. A new-age priest we'd always known in California could do a long weekend. An old friend, Afton, would drive from Los Angeles. *Would it be all right if she brought her seven dogs?* Tom could be here as soon as he got home from the Middle East. A nurse who'd been part of my stepdad's church community could come the weekend I had to go teach a writing workshop in Iowa City. My godmother, Deborah, would come from Monterey. Carmen would fly in from El Salvador.

I bought calendars and dry-erase boards, flowers and dark chocolate, medication logs and cheap wine. I set up the DVD player at the foot of my mother's hospice bed, bought *The Maltese Falcon* and *The Letter* with Bette Davis. I set up the music player. Stacked Cat Stevens, Carol King, Simon and Garfunkel, Joan Baez.

I tried to be honest with my mother's old friends: "If you need to see her alive, come as soon as you can. But if you can hedge your bets, we're probably going to need people for at least a few months." *Was it harsh to put it that way?* I didn't know.

She could live five more years, the oncologist had said, but the palliative care nurse shook her head at that. "Oh, darling," she said, "let's just budget for six months. Your mum's on her journey."

Maxito focused on his pirate Legos. "Beautiful," he kept saying. "Pirates are beautiful."

It was starting to get dark, but no one turned on a light.

Six months. That worked for my brain. I could plan for six months.

The palliative care nurse's cellphone beeped. She read a text from someone, looked up at me. "All right, darling," she said. "They'll bring your mum now." She stood up suddenly, clicked her cowboy boots on the tile floor, grabbed the tape and a rolled-up piece of paper from the table, and unfurled the red and black sign. She marched over to my mother's bedroom door and taped it up. *DNR. Do not resuscitate.*

28.
Pot Stickers at Yummy Café

"I JUST NEED MY MORPHINE PUMP AND A CHECKBOOK," my mother said as the palliative care nurse and the night nurse helped her into her bedroom. *Helped*. Maybe that's a euphemism. They carried her, one on each side.

She wore the loose-fitting Mexican embroidered cottons I'd left for her at the hospital, looked too thin to be wearing them.

I knew people would still call her beautiful, but she had that look of death now – eyes sunken, teeth too prominent.

She'd never asked to come home from the hospital, had in fact refused to leave, but this was how they released people. This was how they released my mother, anyway. The only other option was Casa Que Pasa, the nursing home where the state itself had deemed residents in "immediate jeopardy."

As the nurse-women lifted her into her hospice bed and started hooking up the tubes, my mother gazed at a painting of a crow on the wall. "That's the last painting I bought," she sighed. "It's my friend. My crow. The artist found my crow dead out on the old highway. Think of that. She painted its portrait. She used its bones in art pieces. She buried its organs. She let the river carry away its feathers. Think of all that."

The night nurse's face relaxed into an easy smile. She was smitten. I could tell. And I prayed she would stay smitten, that my mother would stay charming, that everyone who set foot in this house would fall under her spell – fall in love with her – and fucking help me.

My mother glanced at the pile of DVDs, kind of threw her head back to the extent she could throw her head back.

"Do you like old movies?" The night nurse asked.

My mother beamed. "*The Maltese Falcon* is only the greatest screenplay ever written."

I sat down next to her hospice bed, showed her the calendar so far. Leslie would fly in tomorrow evening. Matea, the night nurse, would be here every night at least through the week. Others would come soon. So many people loved her. So many people wanted to come.

My mother stared at me. "You're not going to leave me again, are you, Tiniest?"

The last blue light of evening through the window.

"I won't be here all the time," I admitted. "I'm going to keep my rental. But you'll never be alone. We're making sure you'll never be alone."

My mother nodded. "Okay." She sounded afraid. "I don't want to be a burden." She'd never seemed to mind causing a cyclone of chaos, but there was no glamour in burden. "I should have just blown my brains out," she whispered, too quiet for the nurse-women to hear.

As they arranged pills and pains patches, I ducked into the kitchen to put on a pot of water for tea.

Matea appeared next to me. "Your mother," she said. "She's Frida Kahlo."

My heart swelled with hope. *Yes. Please let my mother stay charming.* "She'd be flattered that you think so," I said. "She's certainly a big Frida fan."

Just then my phone buzzed in my pocket. A text from the chef: *Do you need me to kill your mother yet?*

I texted back: *Not yet.*

She texted again: *Have you eaten?*

I tried to remember. Had I eaten? I hadn't eaten anything that day. Had I eaten anything the day before? I didn't think so. But the hunger was growing on me. I liked the odd comfort of this empty feeling. I didn't know if I wanted to eat. But I knew I wanted the chef.

She was flying to Connecticut in a couple of days to clean out her dad's apartment, to take care of his "affairs," as they say.

I texted back: *Meet you in an hour?*

The ridiculousness of it wasn't lost on me. The mother/daughter/caregiver who couldn't feed herself.

My mother slept, the low hiss of her oxygen machine.

The palliative care nurse gathered her things to leave. "Everything's going to be all right, darling," she said to me.

Matea would call my cell with any news.

I wrote her a check for six hundred dollars for the first three nights, couldn't stop saying "thank you."

I packed up Maxito and his pirate Legos, headed over to Sol's place to leave him for the night. "Is Nonna sick?" he wanted to know. He hadn't seen her, had been playing in the living room, but he was learning to overhear things now.

"Yes, baby," I said. "She's sick. She might die."

Maxito nodded, serious. "One of my chickens died."

"Yes. That was sad."

And he nodded again. "That was so sad."

The chef texted: *Pot stickers at Yummy Café? Or I could cook for you here.*

I felt needy. Uncomfortable in my neediness. It had been exactly one month since her father's death and the chef was worrying about what to feed me. But it struck me as maybe part of my damage, too, the way I dreaded being considered. Maybe I would try an experiment: I would proceed as if being a little bit needy wasn't the worst thing.

If waiting for love wasn't love, maybe love was something different all together than that complicated/elusive thing I'd been trained to wait for. Maybe it was simpler, too. Just some small thing we could use. Like a broken piece of glass, some string. Like an order of pot stickers late at night. Like vegetable broth with bok choi at Yummy Café.

Like a kiss in the chef's gravel driveway and "do you want to come in?"

Like the truth that her question had no double meaning. I could say yes or no without unforeseen consequences.

Like a book of matches.

Like a salted caramel in her palm.

29. *Light* and Other Scattered Words

MY MOTHER DIDN'T WANT A BIBLE IN HER ROOM. SHE didn't want *The Tibetan Book of Living and Dying*. She didn't want Elisabeth Kübler-Ross. She was getting better, dammit, and all this talk about God and science and the afterlife was bumming her out.

Where was Leslie, anyway?

"Here's Leslie."

My sister arrived wearing all white.

I picked her up at the shuttle stop near the train station, stopped with her at Healthy Wealthy for a bouquet of white flowers.

"Leslie," my mother hummed, but then she kind of hissed at her: "Took you long enough." She clung to her morphine pump, smirked even as she hissed.

Leslie smiled. "You thought I'd come faster? Knowing the loving welcome I might expect?"

"I have to pee," my mother sighed. "You have to help me get up to pee."

Leslie untangled the tubes, lifted our mother out of bed and into the bathroom. She stepped just outside the bathroom door, chose the moment to say, "you know, Mom, I got an email from your lawyer. Did you really intend to leave this house to your maid's daughter in Mexico and not to me and Ariel?"

"Oh God," my mother groaned. "I must have been really

mad when I did that. What if I die right here on the toilet before I have a chance to change it?"

"Like Elvis?" Leslie laughed.

"Not funny!" my mother shrieked.

I left them to it.

I had paperwork to attend to. Medical powers of attorney and financial powers of attorney. The man at the bank teared up when I pushed the notarized papers across his desk. "I'm gonna miss her," he said. "You know, sometimes on a slow day, we all just sit around waiting for her to come in and stir up some shit."

It seemed an odd tribute, but what could I say? "I can only imagine."

The banker at the next desk straightened his bright blue tie, looked sad. "Did she ever try to get you fired, man? She tried to get me fired three or four times."

My banker nodded. "Three or four times at least."

"Well, guys," I said. "I'm glad you appreciated her."

I took a mint candy from the bowl. And as I stuffed all the notarized papers back into my turquoise purse, a word fell out: "Light."

I'D BEEN CARRYING all these words around for the last few weeks. Just words on strips of paper. Like cookie fortunes except each paper strip contained just one word.

I'd been dropping them here and there. Not on purpose. Just when I reached into my purse for my lipstick or a few pennies. A word would catch, slip out, fall to the floor.

I started noticing the words here and there. Like a trail of breadcrumbs. Or evidence I'd been someplace before.

The word "monkey" on the chef's dining room table.

I pointed to the word. "Monkey?"

She shrugged. "I don't know where it came from."

I didn't confess that the word was mine.

SEE, I HADN'T been writing through any of this. Wouldn't start writing until summer. I wondered what it meant: A writer who didn't write, walking around with little slips of paper in her purse, scattering words like wildflower seeds, hoping for the best.

One of my first memoir teachers, Floyd Salas back in California, said we could all write stories to convey our single human heart/soul to another human heart/soul and, in doing so, break us both out of our isolation.

But these word-seeds seemed lonely.

"Airplane" taped to the bathroom mirror in my little adobe south of town. I'd been meaning to write a story about a trip I took once, alone. About a time when the world felt expansive.

"Stung" in the grocery store aisle near the shelf with all those fancy bottles of mustard where I stood for so long, trying to decide between the spicy green chile and the organic Dijon.

"Radio" next to my mother's hospice bed.

IN THE KITCHEN of the former duplex, Leslie cooked the things my mother had cooked for us as babies – mashed carrots with parsley and butter, leek and potato soup, banana smoothies. She fed my mother with a tiny silver spoon, filled the freezer with baggies of prepared food to last a couple of weeks. She packed up to leave now, but her son would come next.

In the dim light of the living room, we met with the director of Milagro Home Care. She'd cared for her adult son when he was bed-bound before his death, started her nonprofit. She could send caregivers whenever we needed them. Could we pay twelve dollars an hour? Yes. My mother had a little savings left. We had the social security, too. We could sell the Prius for maybe ten thousand dollars. We could pull this off for a few months.

"It's of course best for our caregivers if you can pay them," she said softly, "but just so you know, if your mother does live a long time, we won't stop coming just because you've run out of money."

I cringed, wanted to assure the woman that we would always figure out how to pay the caregivers, but I remembered my new experiment – to proceed as if a little bit needy wasn't the worst thing. And I said, "thank you."

LESLIE'S TEENAGE SON, Leo, arrived wearing a tie-dyed T-shirt, his hair grown out long after a winter spent camping at Mt. Shasta. He sat with his grandmother in the half-light of her room.

I headed out to meet Carter Quark for a beer at Tomasita's, waited there for the priest from California.

The chef texted Carter from Connecticut as we ordered a second round: *Behave yourself, CQ.*

We laughed at that. I said, "Maybe I'm the one who needs to behave herself." And we laughed harder. Laughed until we cried.

We were waiting for a priest, I'd said, so I guess Carter imagined some Catholic in black. He raised his eyebrows when Carol the new-age earth mama from California stepped in with her cane and flowing cottons.

THE PRIEST AND Leo took turns at my mother's bedside, feeding her and rubbing her feet, taking her to the bathroom.

The lead hospice nurse had frizzy blonde hair with dark roots, came every day to change the bandage on my mother's bed sore. She filled the pill boxes, checked the battery on the morphine pump.

Another hospice worker came on Tuesdays and Fridays, bathed my mother with sponges.

I read the caregiver logs in the mornings. Nights of vomiting and pain. Daily notes that said, "Eve is anxious." Weekly notes that said, "When her friend Moe Hawk visits, she becomes agitated, throws up when Moe Hawk leaves."

"Mom?"

She sat propped in her hospice bed, typing something on her computer.

"Who's Moe Hawk?"

"Oh," my mother sighed. "She's a mental case. She's a white woman who thinks she's Native American."

"Do you want her to keep visiting?"

My mother looked up. "Moe Hawk yells at me. She says I'm not allowed to say I'm dying or I'll die. She says you're all just waiting for me to die. She makes me eat too much."

"We don't have to let her in, Mom."

But my mother shook her head. "Moe Hawk's a mental case, Ariel. You can't fault someone for being a mental case."

THE HOSPICE SOCIAL worker wore a Hawaiian shirt, stood in the kitchen and handed me a list of funeral homes and cremation services. I'd have to pick one, she said, make arrangements before I left town to teach my writing workshop.

"Do you think she'll die in the next couple of days?" I asked the social worker, but she just shrugged.

It seemed crass to make plans for my mother's remains when she was still alive, but I did as I was told, made the calls from my cellphone in the driveway, acted like I was managing. Cremations in Santa Fe cost two to three thousand dollars, but there was a service in Albuquerque where they only charged one thousand. And they could pick up her body here in Santa Fe. *Was it tacky to choose a cut-rate cremation service?* Everything seemed wrong.

A text message from the hospice nurse: *Is it true that Moe Hawk is your mother's sister and authorized to terminate all caregivers?*

I texted back: *Absolutely not. I have no idea where she came from. My mother says she's a mental case. Let's get word to everyone not to leave my mother alone with Moe Hawk.*

THE CHEF POSTED pictures on Facebook. She'd found her dead mother's chemo wig in her dead father's apartment, put it on and started drinking whiskey, taking photos and posting them. Photo after photo.

I texted her: *Come home. You're losing it.*

And she did. Flew home a day early. Knocked on the door of my little adobe just before midnight on Valentine's Day, said "be mine?"

We slept on my couch because I still didn't have a bed. And in the morning, I asked if she was ready to meet the family.

WE CARRIED RED roses into my mother's room, but the room was all a glare. White sunlight too bright.

We sat at my mother's bedside as she drifted in and out.

She seemed confused. "Everything is a dream," she whispered. "Am I dead?"

Leo tried to adjust the curtains, but that strange light wouldn't stop pouring in.

"If I'm dead, I want more flowers," my mother said softly.

The chef carried the bouquets in and out of the room, repositioning the same flowers in different vases.

My mother sighed. "Thank God for all these flowers."

These multiplying flowers.

I wasn't sure if I was self-conscious because of the chef – if I was seeing the scene with outsider eyes – or if my mother did seem suddenly closer to the other side.

I POSTED ON Facebook: *It's getting sketchy here. If any friends who haven't come still want to see my mother, now is the time. I'm sure she'll be available to you in the afterlife, so there's no need for overdramatic travel. But we have life here now.*

"Wow," the chef said as we left. "I'm glad I got to meet her."

It was almost time to pick up Maxito from his new preschool.

"Do you want to meet my boy, too?"

MAXITO RAN CIRCLES around our little table at Yummy Café. We got all the winks and nods, must have looked like some old lesbian couple out for their annual Valentine's dinner with their hyperactive kid – not like two death-soaked daughters on their fourth date.

"Do you think," I asked the chef when the waiter brought Happy Family, "if I go to Iowa, she'll be alive when I get back?"

The chef kind of nodded and shook her head at the same time. "Maybe," she said. But I knew she didn't believe it.

"Do you think I'm a jerk? Leaving?"

The chef shook her head. "No. Definitely not."

The writing workshop I'd scheduled in Iowa City. I could have cancelled it. But I didn't.

NEXT MORNING AND my mother wanted a hug before I left. We weren't huggers – not as mother and daughter – but I leaned over her bed, hugged her for a long time. When I stepped away she was crying. I said, "Are you okay?"

She said, "That's a tall order."

I guess it was. "Is there anything you want to tell me before I go?"

My mother didn't say anything.

"Is there anything you need from me?"

Tears rolled down her face. "It seemed so easy at first," she whispered.

"What does it seem like now?"

She stared at me. "Fix it," she said, and she sort of snapped her fingers.

"What do you want me to fix?"

She snapped her fingers again and said, "fix the email."

I wasn't sure if there was something wrong with her email account, or if she was talking about something metaphorical, but I said, "of course. Consider it fixed."

She closed her eyes, started to drift off, then jerked awake. "Tiniest?"

"Yes?"

"I'm ready."

"Ready for what?"

"I'm ready for *The Tibetan Book of Living and Dying*."

And I said, "All right."

"I don't want any more bullshit." Her tattooed eyeliner seemed so heavy now on her skeletal face. "Tell my friends I'm dying. Put a sign on the door. Tell them I don't want any more bullshit."

I nodded. "No more bullshit."

"Take my makeup bag with you," she said. "Take all the lipstick. I'll never wear it again." But she hesitated, thought better of that, said, "no, wait, leave the makeup. Ronaldo might come and see me. Make the sign and bring me the book, but leave the makeup bag."

I nodded. "Good thinking." When I took a Sharpie out of my purse to make the sign, the word "Clock" caught and fluttered to the tile floor.

"PILLOW" IN THE airport bathroom stall as I was leaving.

"HOME" NEXT TO a dumpster behind a bar in that little Midwestern town I hardly knew.

30.
Poodles and All

IN IOWA, I COOKED FOR STRANGERS. ENCHILADAS WITH Chimayó red chile. Kale and potato salad with onions and capers. I listened to the strangers' stories. Their legacies of love and abuse. I tried not to appear too distracted as I checked my text messages under the table.

At home, my mother vomited. She didn't want to wear the adult diapers, but she could never get to the bathroom in time. Leo or his relief caregiver cleaned up after her, cleaned her, fed her pills even though it hurt her to swallow, even though she vomited most of them. She pressed the morphine button, wet the bed.

"DEATH IS UGLY," my Gammie told me after her last husband died. She poured herself a glass of vodka, tapped her red fingernails on the kitchen counter. "Don't ever let anyone tell you that death isn't ugly."

EXTRAORDINARY TRANSITIONS ARE recounted in the *Tibetan Book of Living and Dying*. The deaths of Buddhist masters, lucid and mystical. But in *How We Die*, the Western doctor Sherwin B. Nuland says that our societal belief in passing with grace and dignity is a collective fantasy. Death, he writes, "is all too frequently a series of destructive events that involve by their very nature the disintegration of the dying person's humanity. I have not often seen much dignity in the process by which we die." In fact, "The quest to achieve true dignity fails when our bodies fail. Occasionally–very occasionally–unique circumstances of death will be granted to someone with a unique personality, and that lucky combination will make it happen, but such a confluence of fortune is uncommon, and, in any case, not to be expected by any but a very few people."

I didn't expect my mother to die like some enlightened monk.

MY LAST MORNING in Iowa, my host, Shell, fed me dark chocolate for breakfast before she drove me to the Cedar Rapids airport. "Look," she pointed to the sky. "That cloud with the sun behind it looks like a cross."

It did. "Like God."

My mother was alive when I got on the plane headed home.

She was alive when I landed in Albuquerque.

I stepped into her room, gagged at the smell. Putrid, like decomposing compost.

She smiled weakly from her bed, asked "how much longer?"

Leo had the window open, but it was cold outside. The heater blasted.

"I don't know how much longer, Mom."

She curled her finger at me.

I moved closer.

"You have to kill me, Ariel," she whispered.

I shook my head. I wasn't going to be the one to kill her. It had been crazy-making enough being her daughter for 41 years. I certainly wasn't going to kill her. "I can't help you with that," is all I said.

IN THE DINING room, the hospice nurse fretted about my mother's anxiety medication. *Why were these extra pills here? Had she missed a dose?*

"What can we do about the smell in there?" I asked.

The nurse frowned, scratched her eyebrow. "It's the rotting

flesh around your mother's bed sore. It's tunneling in. The spine is exposed. Do you want to see it?"

I didn't want to see it.

"That bedsore is the only imminently life threatening thing we're dealing with right now," the nurse said. "As far as the smell goes, you can try putting half an onion in the room. And an open box of baking soda under the bed. You probably shouldn't let her see you do it. She might be embarrassed. Just put the onion in the wastebasket and the baking soda under the bed. Put a new half onion in the wastebasket every day."

Another task to add to the front of the logbook.

LESLIE'S EX-BOYFRIEND ARRIVED for his weeklong ministry, lanked around the house talking incessantly about sex and orgasm. He sautéed marijuana in butter, fed that to my mother. And now there were no further mentions of vomiting in the log.

After a month of baby food, Leslie's ex had my mother eating bread with olive oil, baked tilapia, and spinach quiche, but he seemed overwhelmed with all the medications. He scratched his head. "You can tell you've missed a dose when she gets really agitated."

My mother had been home from the hospital for a month. I called Milagro Home Care, told them we needed caregivers 24–7 now. Friends would still come to help, but it was all too much for a single untrained person.

"TINIEST," MY MOTHER smiled when I walked into her room. "I dreamed you brought me a gleaming woman. Bathed in light, she had silver hair."

I texted the chef: *I think my mother is asking for you.*

When the chef showed up maybe twenty minutes later, my mother gasped. "I thought I dreamed you."

She smiled shy. "I've been told I'm too good to be true." And she sat next to the hospice bed, talked with my mother about food and Mexico, asked if there was anything she'd like to eat.

"Well, yes," my mother said. "Ceviche with red snapper. Miso soup. Oaxacan molé. Can you make those things?"

"I can make anything," the chef said.

"Can we have an Oscar party?" my mother asked, wide-eyed.

"Sure. This Sunday?"

My mother smiled. "Can you make Chinese food?"

"Yes. I used to own an Asian restaurant."

"Chef?" my mother whispered. "Whatever happens between you and Ariel, I'm leaving you the kitchen."

A knock at the open front door. It seemed like someone was always knocking at the door now.

I left my mother and the chef to their hospice menu plans.

A young guy stood on the front step, a green backpack slung over his shoulder.

"Can I help you?"

"Yeah," he shrugged. "I was just passing through town and I saw the door was open."

I stared at him.

He smiled. "I'm just kidding. They sent me? From Milagro?"

I'd forgotten. "Yes, sorry. Come in."

"I'm Cloud," he said, and he sat down at the dining room table to read the caregiver log to date. We had my mother's medication schedule and urgent messages in the front of the binder, then the daily notes. "Well," he said when he was done with it. "What we need here is a diagnosis and a short biography so that any time anyone comes in here they can sit down and read this and have both the overview and the day-by-day picture and be ready to go."

"All right," I said, and I sat down with Cloud and set to work transforming the log into something comprehensive.

OVER THE DAYS, the caregivers came. They were nursing students or underemployed health care workers, massage therapists or aspiring herbalists. They wrote their names on a dry-erase board in my mother's room so she'd feel less disoriented.

THEY MADE NOTES in the log:

> *12:40 p.m. Eve is falling asleep now.*
>
> *6:25 p.m. Vomiting and pain on right side of chest. Called lead nurse to change battery in morphine pump.*
>
> *7:30 p.m. Eve wants to watch "Strangers on a Train."*
>
> *9:20 p.m. "The Maltese Falcon" (again).*
>
> *2:15 a.m. Eve is awake, nauseous, in pain, disoriented, anxious, angry.*
>
> *5:20 a.m. Eve said she had to go to the bathroom, sat on toilet for one hour, said she couldn't go. As I lifted her up she had an accident on the floor. Cleaned up.*
>
> *11:45 a.m. Eve awake, eating spinach and garbanzo beans, alert, happy.*

FOR THE OSCAR party, the chef made scallop ceviche for my mother. She made the Chinese food, too: Summer rolls and bok choi, scallion pancakes with hoisin sauce, pork tenderloin and shrimp shu mai.

Maia flew in for the weekend.

Maxito adjusted the lights.

And we all sat on pillows around my mother's hospice bed as *The Artist* and *Hugo* won the statues. She said, "All this is heavenly," then cried, "I can't believe I never wrote my screenplay," she trailed off, "never won my Oscar ..."

"YOUR MOTHER ISN'T following any of the normal patterns," the lead hospice nurse said when I arrived the next day. "We could be here for many months."

I washed dishes, scanned the log, opened a bar of dark chile chocolate.

"Normally a patient might go from soft foods to liquids. Then she might start refusing food all together. That would tell us she had just a few days. But your mother has graduated from soft foods to complex solid foods, and ..." she bit her lip. "The bedsore is beginning to heal."

"That's good, right?"

The hospice nurse nodded. "It's unbelievable."

I popped a piece of spicy chocolate into my mouth. I believed it. With all the marijuana Leslie's ex was feeding her and the chef's food – why wouldn't we get a miracle?

THE CHEF WAS in my mother's kitchen making miso soup for the week when another prospective caregiver knocked on the open door.

We didn't usually interview caregivers. Milagro Home Care just sent them over and I wrote the checks. But this one, Sherman, said he had some questions for us.

"Sure," I said. "Come in."

He wore a zebra-print jacket and white leather boots, smelled like cigarettes. "Well," he puckered. "I have some needs. I'm wondering if I can bring my two poodles with me."

It occurred to me that Leslie or Maia had somehow had this guy sent over from Central Casting, that we were being punked.

"Poodles?"

"Yes, you know, I used to be a poodle groomer? In Hollywood?" He flicked his wrist. "Can I meet your mother?"

I led him into my mother's room where she sat with Cloud. She liked Cloud, but she always called him Ocean or Storm or Mist. He didn't seem to mind. One weather-related noun was as good as the next.

"SERIOUSLY?" THE CHEF said when I stepped back into the kitchen. "Poodles?"

I dialed Milagro Home Care, said we could do without Sherman and his needs, but after he'd left my mother shrieked, "How could you send him away? He's a Hollywood hairdresser. He's going to do my hair!"

"He's a poodle groomer, Mom. It's different."

She glared at me. "I want Sherman."

So I dialed again, told the scheduler I'd misspoken. We wanted Sherman after all. We wanted Sherman, poodles and all.

31. My Mother's Memoir

"I KNOW WHERE I WAS BORN." MY MOTHER SAT IN BED with her laptop and cried, kept crying. "I was born at Cedars-Sinai Hospital on November tenth, nineteen forty one. I know where I was born."

I'd closed her bedroom door behind me, but the poodles whined and scratched at the door. "Of course you know where you were born, Mom." I lifted the computer from her lap, sat down in the chair next to her bed.

She'd forgotten her email password again and this was the security question. *In which hospital were you born?* I tried every variation I could think of: *Cedars-Sinai, Cedars Sinai* without the dash, *Cedars-Sinai Hospital, Cedars-Sinai Medical Center.*

Her shoulders shook as she cried. "I know where I was born."

I Googled "other names for Cedars-Sinai," scrolled through the Wikipedia article. In 1941, Cedars-Sinai was called Cedars of Lebanon. "Cedars of Lebanon?" I whispered.

"Yes," she wept now, her whole body convulsing. "That's what I said. I was born at Cedars of Lebanon."

"Of course you were." I typed it in, *Cedars of Lebanon*, reset the fucking password. "We got it. It's all right."

In a few minutes her breath began to steady. "I was born at Cedars of Lebanon on November tenth, nineteen forty one."

AS MY MOTHER checked her email, I sat watching the wall, scrolled through the to-do list in my mind. All the work I had to catch up on. My online class. My ghostwriting deadline.

WHEN I WAS a little girl I wanted nothing more than my mother's attention. My beautiful mother. But she had more important people and things to attend to. Now I sat with her dying, sat steeped in boredom.

MY MOTHER PRESSED her morphine pump, looked up from her computer. "Did you bring me a book about writing memoir or did I dream it?"

"I think you dreamed it."

"You teach memoir writing, don't you?"

I nodded. "Yes. That's what I do."

She half-closed her eyes, pushed the morphine button again. "Do you think memoir writing is a way to express anger or a way to pay tribute?"

I'd never thought about it in those terms. "Maybe both," I said.

My mother nodded. "At what age do people discover philosophy?"

I thought about that. "Around fourteen?" I guessed. "That first crisis of meaning. Younger if they're abused."

She narrowed her eyes at me. "Were you abused?"

I rubbed my forehead. "Sometimes I think of it that way."

"*I* was abused," she said.

"I know." I picked up her sippy cup of water for her.

"Can I tell you a story, Tiniest? For my memoir? I'm too tired to type."

"Sure." I took the laptop from her. "I can type it."

So my mother told me a story.

"ONCE UPON A time, Tiniest," my mother started. She gazed up at her crow painting on the far wall. "A little girl went missing." She swallowed. "That's how you start a story, isn't it, Tiniest?"

"Sure," I said.

And she coughed. "It was the first time I'd ever heard of such a thing. Of missing children. I was seven years old and we lived in G.I. housing in the Pacific Palisades. On Temecula Avenue. Almost all the houses had the same floor plan. For years I could still remember that little girl's name, but I've forgotten it now. She was the same age as me. Search parties went out looking for her."

My mother shifted, looked out the window. "I was terrified the little girl had fallen into one of the open trenches in the neighborhood – they were everywhere, the trenches dug for the sewer pipes. It was scary to look into those trenches. They were deep and narrow and muddy."

My mother pressed her morphine button. "There were incinerators in people's back yards. We burned our own trash in those days. Everything that could be burned. My father was just back from the war – he'd been a pilot, his plane downed in the South Pacific, he'd been a POW – and now he'd cram the incinerator full and he'd throw in burning kindling and pretty soon his fire raged and raged in its concrete container and he'd pick me up in his thick hands and he'd hold me over that roaring fire and he'd say, "You want to go in there, Evie?" and he'd motion to throw me in.

"I screamed and clung to him, but I was so scared, the "no" hardly came out. Madre couldn't hear me. I knew she couldn't hear me. I only had the person who would throw me into the fire to cling to. I understood that."

My mother didn't cry or smile as she told me her story, just kept watching her crow, pushing the morphine button.

I'd read someplace that it takes four generations to recover from war. By this math, and assuming no further deployments, Maia and Maxito's children might be free.

My mother coughed. "One day they found the body of the little girl who'd been missing. They found her in one of those deep muddy ditches. She'd fallen in and died. I wish I could tell you her name."

The hiss of the oxygen tank.

"That's sad," I said.

But my mother shook her head, scolded me: "It's more than sad, Tiniest. It's a lie. I spent my whole childhood terrified of those trenches, of falling, but that little girl didn't fall. Little whatever-her-name-was. Someone murdered her, obviously, and they disposed of her body, just threw her into the sewer. Evil doesn't just happen, Tiniest. People don't just fall into the earth like that. Evil is what we do to each other." She closed her eyes. "It's what we do."

I sat there at her bedside, watched the rise and fall of her chest as she breathed through her oxygen tube. I sat there until I knew she was asleep. And then I crept out, quiet as I could, the way you do when you've just put a baby down.

I SAT AT the medicine desk we'd set up in the laundry room, wrote checks to the caregivers. We couldn't afford the 24–7 help forever. Abra had suggested giving notice on our little adobe outside of town, the two of us and Maxito moving back in to the former duplex. My mother said she liked that idea. She wanted us here with her. But I wasn't ready for this house to be the only home I had.

I took my mother's car keys from a basket on the kitchen counter, poked my head into her room. "Mind if I sell the Prius?"

She smiled weakly, resigned to it. "Sure," she said. "Don't get ripped off."

The Prius would buy us another month of caregivers.

THAT NIGHT I sat on the porch of my old adobe, cracked open a State Pen Porter. My phone buzzed. My mother's landline.

"Tiniest," she whispered. "You have to fire Sherman."

"All right," I said. "Any particular reason?" I sipped my beer, imaged he'd done her hair up like a poodle's.

But my mother sounded stricken. "He found my morphine stash, Tiniest. I had enough to end this. Sherman told on me. They took it. Who does that? He told on me."

"I'm sorry," I said, and knocked back the rest of my beer. "Consider him fired."

I didn't have Maxito that night, so I curled onto my bedroll with a copy of *Rose: Love in Violent Times*. Maybe all times were violent times.

"CAN THE LAST part of my memoir be a screenplay?" my mother asked as soon as I stepped into her room the next day. She'd been pushing her morphine pump twice as much as usual, according to the log, but the thing had its programmed limit.

My mother's memoir seemed a harmless enough project, but a part of me felt like a cad for humoring her. We only had a few pages so far. There would be no book, no movie. Still, I said, "a screenplay? Sure."

She smiled. "Not too unconventional?"

"I think it could be interesting," I said. "Multimedia."

Cloud brought my mother a cup of herbal tea, set it on her bedside table.

Her hand shook as she lifted the cup, but she took a sip. "What do you know about trauma, Ariel?"

This was one of those questions my mother often asked me, not because she wanted to hear what I knew about trauma from my own experience, but rather she wanted to be sure I'd been listening to her all my life, that I'd been learning these things she considered imperative.

There were right and wrong answers to questions like this one.

Eve-family pop quiz.

I knew from trauma, knew from being kicked in the ribs when I'd expected a lover's tenderness, knew from standing in front of a family court judge waiting for the decree that would tell me whether or not I was fit to be a mother. But I also knew that the correct answer now was something more academic. "Trauma," I said, "by its very definition, can't be fully experienced in the moment. Due to the suddenness or the enormity of the traumatic event, we just can't take it in. So we have to go back to it at some point – either literally or symbolically – to integrate whatever happened. We can do that consciously, in some safe way, or we're destined to revisit the trauma over and over again as the violence of life."

My mother nodded. This was the right answer. "What do you know about abuse, Ariel?" *Pop quiz question number two*.

I knew something about abuse, too, knew sexual violence and jagged steel keys bashing into a naked forehead. I knew words chosen solely to make a person feel worthless and crazy. But I knew the answer to this question, too. "Abuse needs a witness," I said, "either in the immediate present moment or revisited later – like in some kind of therapy or confessional – if there's to be any hope of healing."

My mother nodded. I was two for two. "What do you know about evil, Tiniest?"

I didn't answer. I had some ideas about evil. And I knew she wanted me to tell her about Bobbie Harris back at San Quentin. About the way he was beaten out of the womb. About the way he killed those boys, but that's not what got him the death penalty. About the way he ate their leftover hamburgers after he shot them. About that's what made him cold blooded. But I stayed silent. I was getting tired of this game.

My mother gazed out the window, looked so sad. "John died all wrong," she said.

John. My stepdad. The priest. The one she killed unless they were in on it together.

"What do you mean all wrong?"

She was quiet for a long time. "We talked about it," she finally said, "but when I gave him the poison it was all wrong. I didn't feel anything. I should have taken the poison too. I should have lain down with him and died. But I just gave him the poison. I went into the living room and I turned on the TV and watched Anderson Cooper. Just like some cold-blooded killer."

Cloud peeked around the door frame just then. "Ronaldo's here," he said.

And my mother gasped. "Tiniest, My hair– "

"Give us a minute," I whispered to Cloud.

"Sure thing."

I BRUSHED MY mother's gray hair, fastened a silver comb to keep it from her face. I filed her nails, took the blush from her make-up bag and dusted her cheeks.

"I just need to look alive," she whispered.

"Lipstick?"

She smiled at me. "That would just look fake, Tiniest. I want to look natural for Ronaldo."

32.
Seven Swords

I LET MAXITO SLEEP IN.

It must have been after 9 a.m. when he finally tip-toed into the kitchen of the little adobe, rosy-cheeked and rubbing his eyes. "Good morning," he said. "I want a sandwich." He squinted against the morning sun. "And let's make you some coffee, Mama."

He stood up on his wooden step stool and I watched his little hands as he pressed the button to grind the coffee beans for me.

I remembered when I was pregnant with Maia how terrified I felt that I would abuse her. That I would torment her. And I remembered the flood of relief when I realized unabusive motherhood wasn't so very hard. That sure – it took a diligence, probably more diligence when emotional violence was my first language. But that in the end it isn't so hard not to ruin everything we love. It meant deferring to my child when I felt that wit's-end rage bubble up, meant stepping back to remind myself that she was the baby here, that I was the grown-up. It meant reminding myself to behave in a way I would be proud of. It meant not always needing to be right, apologizing when I was wrong. It meant a lot of pause-taking. But it wasn't so very hard.

I made Maxito a banana sandwich.

We sat outside. The first warm morning in March.

He fed his bread crusts to the chickens, climbed the

branches of the plum tree he called his own. A blossom. “It’s getting springtime,” he said. “I love being in a tree.”

I should have had him at daycare two hours earlier, but I liked it here in the late warm morning. Just feeding the chickens. Pretending we didn’t have anyone else to care for.

MY BUDDHIST FRIEND in Albuquerque texted me the name of a gym she knew in Santa Fe. She wanted me to start lifting weights, she said. She wanted me to stay strong. And have you tried going to the dump and breaking plates? It might be a good way to get any anger out of your body without hurting anyone. She was meditating, she said, on swords that cut through delusions and into the heart of things.

I texted my Buddhist friend back: *I think I’m learning something about those swords.*

And now the chef texted: *I want to get my African violets colored in. Tattoo date?*

My stars had healed.

Yes. I wanted more.

What was a tattoo anyway, but a visual reminder of pain and healing. The memoir inked into our skin. Some symbolic way to integrate the enormity of everything.

I grabbed one of the three copies of the new Clarissa Pinkola Estés’ book I’d gotten for Christmas, remembered an image of the pierced heart of Mary somewhere in those pages. “The swords through your heart are not the ones that caused your wounds, but rather, these swords of strength were earned by your struggle through hard times.”

Here it was, “the unruined heart” pierced by seven swords. I didn’t think I’d earned all those swords yet, but maybe the pierced/unruined heart could become some self-fulfilling prophecy. Like *right now I insist that right now some beautiful girl is sitting on the bank of a river with a copy of this book in her hands and right now she has a rose in her hair.*

I texted the chef back: *Yes, please. Tattoo date.*

MY MOTHERS' ESTRANGED best friend's daughter was flying in that night. Karin. She would sit by my mother's hospice bed, read her Mary Oliver poetry. She would sing to her. She would pour me a glass of wine in the custom kitchen, shake her head, and say, "this is intense – dark and spirit-filled work – I don't know how you're doing it."

I didn't know if I was doing it.

MAIA ARRIVED FOR a long weekend.

My mother wept at the sight of her, pointed to the crow painting on her wall, "my crow," she told Maia. "It makes me cry."

Maia sat with her, read her passages from a book by the painting-artist about that crow until my mother fell asleep.

A FACEBOOK MESSAGE from my old friend Teagan: *What does it mean for life to bear witness to death?*

I didn't answer her, didn't want to answer her. Even Baba Yaga said that not all questions cry out to be answered. I just messaged back: *You're gonna start quoting Freud on me now?*

What did it mean for life to bear witness to death? My oracle back in Portland had said I could ask questions after a year, but it occurred to me now that it didn't promise any good answers.

IN THE YARD behind the former duplex, the living crows had started to gather. Five of them on the back fence. The snow fell. Ten of them now. It kept falling. There must have been thirty crows in the trees and on that back fence come first day of spring.

"Are there always so many crows in your backyard?" my Buddhist friend from Albuquerque asked when she stopped by to paint my fingernails purple.

"No. They've been gathering."

And now here was my mother on the new caregiver Octavio's arm. She hadn't been out of bed in a month. She wrinkled her nose at the bottles of nail polish on the dining room table. "Are you trying to kill me? With those fumes?"

"I can't believe you're up, Mom. That's great."

She stood unsteady, leaned into Octavio, said, "Do you know what I want? I want a pumpkin chiffon pie. Just like Madre used to make."

Madre. My Gammie. Her pumpkin chiffon pie.

I actually had the recipe. "You got it," I said. "Pumpkin chiffon pie."

THE NEXT DAY I stepped into my mother's room, carrying my ugly little pumpkin chiffon pie. I couldn't find the right ginger snaps at Healthy Wealthy for the crust, had been too impatient to let the pumpkin and egg white mixture cool properly. That pie smelled perfect, but it didn't look like anything Gammie would have served.

"I hate you!" my mother shrieked.

I set the pie down on her desk, between the TV stand and the painting of the crow. "Okay, Mom. I give up, why do you hate me?"

"I'm not ready to die," she screamed. "Who does that? Who doesn't get ready to die? Do you want to know why I hate you, Tiniest?"

"Sure." I was so tired.

"You've got everything and I've got nothing, all right? There you have it. You have a life and I don't have a life."

I shook my head, wanted to take a handful of that pie and cram it down her throat.

"You've always had a life, all right?" my mother seethed. "I'm a jealous bitch. That's the truth about your mother. Your mother's a jealous bitch. Are you happy now?"

"Yes, Mom," I said. "I'm bubbling over with glee. This is exactly the kind of conversation I always dreamed of having with you on your deathbed." I left her with her pie.

"Tiniest?" she called after me.

I didn't answer.

"Is that a pie?" she yelled.

I didn't answer.

"Oh my God, Tiniest," my mother cried. "You made me the pie."

I GRABBED A pile of white dishes from my mother's kitchen, texted the chef from the driveway: *Can we get out of town for a couple of days?*

Maxito would be with Sol anyway.

The chef texted back: *Yes, definitely*.

On the way home to my little adobe, I stopped at the dump, stood at the edge of the garbage pit and held each plate, one by one, smooth in my hands, before I raised it above my head and hurled it into the pit. The sound of the ceramic hitting concrete.

AT HOME I packed fast. The chef picked me up in her gold Jeep and we drove south down Highway 25, drove toward the lithium hot springs in Truth or Consequences.

We'd hole up in a room with a hot plate and a private mineral bath through April Fools' Day.

"My mother is never going to die," I mumbled.

It had been two months since her release from the hospital.

My friends on Facebook threw virtual confetti. *Death is beautiful!* they insisted, and *This is your time with her!*

How could I explain the depth of my exhaustion? I knew I should be living in the present, in these ugly and sacred moments. I thought of the little girl clinging to her father as he held her over the fire, clinging because he was all she had. But I was glad my mother wasn't all I had.

IN *THE TIBETAN Book of Living and Dying*, Sogyal Rinpoche recalls the death of a spiritual master. He was just seven years old when he witnessed it: The old man beckoned one of his students to his side. "A-mi," he called her, my child. "Come here," he said. "It's happening now. I've no further advice for you. You are fine as you are: I am happy with you."

WE KEPT DRIVING fast south in the chef's Jeep. I never thought my mother would die with the grace of a master, but now I made quick peace with the possibility that my last conversation with her might have been the one about how much she hated me.

My phone buzzed with a call. I wanted to ignore it. My mother's landline. "Hello?"

"Tiniest?" she whispered, anxious. "You have to come here now."

"I can't, Mom." I watched out the Jeep window. Citizen Cope on the car stereo. I watched all that dry red earth, watched the dry river beds as we crossed over each bridge.

My mother's voice, frantic: "Someone put a Post-it Note on the faux finished cabinets in the kitchen, Tiniest."

This was her problem. A Post-it Note.

I'd seen it, actually. The note. A missive about which organic beans my mother liked better. (Pinto, not black).

"They've *ruined* the paint job, Tiniest. A person who would put a Post-it on my faux finishing would do *anything*," my mother cried. "You have to find out who's done this." Her voice cracked. "You have to fire whoever's done this. Don't let them anywhere near me. Please. Don't let *anyone* who would do *anything* like this anywhere *near* me."

"All right," I promised on the phone, clicked it off. The low desert shrubs. I texted all the caregivers: *Don't anyone admit to putting the Post-it Note on the faux finishing.*

33.
The Heart Sutra

MY CELLPHONE RANG TOO EARLY IN THE MORNING. A number I only vaguely recognized. I let it go to voicemail, crawled out from under the quilts of my bedroll, crept into the kitchen to make myself a cup of coffee.

Outside the kitchen window, a dusting of snow. The snow still coming down.

Abra had fallen asleep on the couch.

My kitchen lights flickered off. On again.

The sound of the kettle whistle.

Abra sat up, tired. "How will we look back on these days, Lady Yaga?"

I glanced up at the painting of the winged house. "With relief that they're over and some odd wish we could go back and do it all better."

I liked the way that Abra was still young enough to think of me as an oracle.

I grabbed a blanket, took my coffee out onto the front porch, dialed voicemail for the message.

A shaky voice. Lara. One of the newer caregivers from Milagro. "Ariel, you need to come up to the house right now." A silence. "Your mother is passing today. All the signs are here."

I didn't call Lara back, just finished my coffee, ducked back inside, threw on a pair of jeans and a sweater, pulled on my boots, didn't tell Abra the why of my sudden hurry.

I made an egg sandwich for Maxito, stuffed his clothes into

my purse, lifted him out of his bed in his pajamas, whispered, "we have to go to daycare a little bit early today, sweetie."

As I buckled him into his car seat, he smiled sleepy.

I handed over the egg sandwich, drove toward town, drove into the building blizzard, tried not to drive too fast, probably drove too fast.

Your mother is passing today. Most of me knew I didn't have to be there when she passed, but the world seemed to want me there. *You need to come up to the house right now.*

I dropped Maxito off at his new daycare, helped him brush his teeth in the school bathroom before circle time, made my way to the house. Lara hugged me when I stepped into the entryway, hugged me for so long I wondered if my mother had already died.

But Lara led me into my mother's room. She lay there on her back, mouth open. I watched her chest. Her breath. Life or death. She was a skeleton in her purple T-shirt and silk leopard-print robe. The hiss of oxygen. The rise and fall. She was alive.

I sat down next to her. Sat there for a long time.

Lara sat next to me, said, "I've been doing this work for years. This is your mother's day."

I didn't want to argue with a professional, but I said, "my mother will surprise you." Then I doubted myself. Maybe I was just jaded to death dates. "Should we put on some music?"

Lara put on a CD. Buddhist chanting. The heart sutra. She turned the volume down to a whisper. And the two of us just sat there, kept sitting:

> All things are empty:
> Nothing is born, nothing dies,
> nothing is pure, nothing is stained,
> nothing increases and nothing decreases.
> So, in emptiness, there is no body ...

I THOUGHT ABOUT Gammie. No one sat with her as she died. She lived alone. Ninety-one years old. She just got up in the middle of the night to pour herself a glass of milk and bourbon and she fell down. I missed her, my Gammie. Wanted to call her now. Ask her what I should do:

> There is no ignorance,
> and no end to ignorance.
> There is no old age and death,
> and no end to old age and death.
> There is no suffering, no cause of suffering...

MY MOTHER OPENED her eyes and jerked up, stared at the two of us siting there. The whisper of the heart sutra, the hiss of oxygen. "What? Did you think I was dead? I want an omelet." She shook her head and cackled. "Someone make me a fucking omelet."

I CRACKED EGGS in my mother's kitchen, whispered to Lara, "What were the signs? That made you think she would die today?"

Lara chopped herbs. "The lights flickered," she said softly.

I thought about that. *Was she kidding?* "The lights flickered at my little place south of town, too," I said. "There's actually a blizzard." I flipped the omelet.

34.
Moveable Feasts

"TINIEST," MY MOTHER STARTED WHEN I STEPPED INTO her room. "Matea tells me it's Passover. We have to prepare a Seder. The leg of lamb. All the dishes. The bitter herb. Maxito can ask the questions."

I shook my head, set a cup of herbal tea on her bedside table. "First of all, Mom, we're not Jewish. And anyway it's too late to do a Seder." We sometimes celebrated Passover when I was a kid, but it was already past 6 p.m. and we didn't have any matzo. "Listen," I said. "Easter's in a couple of days. Let's do Easter. The chef wants to cook for you again. Anything you crave. Traditional or not."

"Okay," my mother smiled. "Sit down with me. We'll make the menu."

MY MOTHER WANTED leg of lamb with mint jelly and gravy. She wanted red wine, some good pairing. *Did the chef know about wine pairings?* Of course. My mother wanted fancy ginger ale. *Had I tried Q Ginger Ale?* No, but I'd get it. She wanted salad, rosemary potatoes, roasted asparagus, carrot cupcakes with cream cheese frosting.

"What else should we have, Tiniest?"

"I think it sounds perfect," I said. "We can get a plane ticket for Leslie to come too."

My mother brightened. "And Maia?"

Maia had already missed too many Monday classes with

her weekend visits. "She has midterms," I said. "She'll come again soon."

"And Maxito?"

"Yes. Maxito."

"We'll make him an Easter basket," she smiled, tears in her eyes. "With real flowers." She pressed her morphine button.

"Yes. Let's."

THE CHEF AND I made the grocery list and pushed through the aisles of Healthy Wealthy. Early afternoon on Easter and we stood in the chef's little kitchen organizing ingredients. I recognized the nurse Matea's number on my cellphone. She worked for both hospice and Milagro Home Care now. "Hello?"

"Are you in town, Ariel?"

"Yes?"

"You should come up to the house," Matea said. "You should come now."

I swallowed hard. "What's up?"

But Matea just said, "Your mother isn't doing that well."

4/8/12
8:00 a.m. Eve woke happy, washed up in bathroom, ate toast & fruit & yogurt with tea. Had her meds.

10:00 a.m. Matea arrived to change the dressing on the bedsore, new sores starting where adhesive is. Matea went for more bandages. Eve sat for an hour at breakfast. New red patches began to appear. Will encourage her to sit only for short periods.

11:25 a.m. Eve is happy, animated, wants to get up and check the guest room to make sure it's ready and clean for Leslie.

THE CHEF FOLLOWED me into my mother's kitchen, set down the bags from Healthy Wealthy.

Matea stood with a woman I'd never seen before, started crying. "Ariel," she said. "I'm so sorry."

The new woman started crying, too. She was thin, with

desert-colored hair. "I tried to resuscitate her. I know she was DNR, but it's *Easter*. She was so looking forward to her feast."

I glanced out the window. All those living crows had taken flight. I wondered how deep we'd have to dig to reach well water, wondered that just then for no reason.

What does it mean for life to bear witness to death?

I stepped into my mother's room alone.

She wore her silk leopard-print robe. Lay there as if asleep, mouth slightly open, some peaceful portrait of herself. And even I couldn't help but notice then that she was beautiful.

I sat in the chair next to her hospice bed, sat there with her for just a few minutes, thought to take her hand and then didn't. "Well," I finally said to her, "I think we did all right in the end, don't you? Behaved in a way we can be *sorta* proud of? I mean. You built a beautiful kitchen. And I didn't kill you."

MY MOTHER'S CROW watched silent from the wall as Matea and the new woman washed her body.

I stood for a long time in her closet, forgetting and remembering my task: to pick out the clean white Mexican cottons she would wear to the incinerator.

The women dressed her, placed a red glass heart on her chest and flowers by her arms. They wrapped her head and jaw in a white scarf to keep her mouth closed, turned the heat down in the room to ward off the smell of death.

The undertaker would come for her body in the morning.

THE CHEF UNWRAPPED the leg of lamb, peeled russet potatoes, cut asparagus.

I crept in and out of my mother's room, bringing white candles, half-expecting to notice the subtle rise and fall of her chest, half-expecting her to sit up suddenly and demand an omelet. But the sunlight waned into evening as it does, and my mother's skin looked only paler, her body ever still.

IN THE CUSTOM kitchen, the chef sprinkled rosemary on the potatoes, tossed radicchio in lemon-mustard dressing, melted butter, opened the wine.

Leslie landed at the Albuquerque airport, would catch a shuttle.

Abra crossed the Colorado border on her way home from Spring break.

Maia cried on the phone, made plane reservations for the following weekend.

I left a message for Sol not to bring Maxito after all.

AND I SET the table with my Gammie's silver, set a place for my mother, too, poured her a glass of red Zinfandel, let the chair sit empty the way we used to at our un-Jewish Seders – a place for the prophet Elijah, should he happen to stop by.

35.
Kitchen World

THE CHEF STUDIED THE NOTES IN MY MOTHER'S OAXACAN cookbooks, ad-libbed the menu for the memorial spread: Mole chichilo with chicken and chayote squash, pork and guajillo chile tamales, black bean and cotija cheese tamales, fresh tortillas, cabbage and serrano salad, arroz verde, calabacitas.

We'd only given ourselves a week to pull together a service. We had to get to work.

The chef roasted and seeded and soaked the ancho chiles, the mulato, the casacabel, the pasilla negro, the chile de arbol, the guajillo, the costeño, and the New Mexico red.

We taught Maxito to peel garlic and he stood on his little stepping stool, concentrating hard as he slipped the skin off each clove.

The chef helped him press cooked tomatoes and tomatillos though a strainer, separating the skins and seeds from the juice and pulp.

Maxito said, "I see. We like this part. We don't like that part."

We posted pictures on Facebook and my friend China commented: *Life is so hard sometimes. But you all really know how to live. You get together. You cook.*

I wasn't sure we knew how to live, but maybe we were learning; withstanding this time of learning. We were getting together, cooking, taking respite from the big world of death and meanness in this smaller kitchen-world where things made sense, where if we gathered the right ingredients and had the patience, things turned out the way we thought they would.

LILIES ARRIVED FROM relatives and friends and I lined them up along the walls of the house, vase after vase.

The chef soaked beans, cooked the chile base, the pork.

Leo had been camping with some friends outside of Truth or Consequences, so Leslie borrowed a car and headed south to retrieve him. They'd stop at the cut-rate cremation service in Albuquerque on their way back, pick up my mother's ashes.

Abra ordained herself online and paged through The Bible and *The Tibetan Book of Living and Dying* and Mary Oliver poetry collections looking for the passages she would read aloud at the service.

My mother had left no instructions, so we made it all up as we went along. Improvising this death.

I STOOD IN line at Healthy Wealthy, a dozen bottles of wine and compostable wine glasses made of corn on the conveyor belt.

"I know what you're doing!" a henna redhead squealed when she saw my haul. "You're having an art opening!"

"Guess again," I mumbled.

"A reception?" she chirped.

"Try again."

ON MY WAY to the copy shop to make memorial programs I noticed a homemade poster glued to a utility box. "St. Henry Miller of Words," it read. A black-ink portrait of the old guy and the quote, "The one thing we can never give enough of is love ... and the only thing we never give enough of is love."

Henry Miller. Maybe Eve was with him by now.

THE MILAGRO CAREGIVER Octavio appeared in the open doorway. "I came by to pick up my check," he said, then scanned all those white bouquets. "I guess I missed something."

"Yes," I told him. "She died on Easter."

Octavio nodded, quiet. His skin was pockmarked. "Who killed her?"

I shrugged. "I think she just died. I think her heart gave out."

Octavio scratched his chin. "She was asking everyone to kill her. Someone must have killed her."

I wrote a check, held it out to him.

"Who killed her?" He asked again.

But I shook my head. "Octavio, not every question cries out to be answered."

YOU KNOW, IN that old Russian story Vasilisa the Wise, Baba Yaga doesn't kidnap the girl. Vasilisa goes to the witch's house voluntarily – no idea what she's getting into, but she does go voluntarily. She goes seeking light.

Vasilisa knows enough to know that not every question needs to be asked, that not every question has a good answer. And Vasilisa walks out of Baba Yaga's place completely unscathed. She walks out carrying the light that will burn through all the complicated violence she's been taught to call love.

OCTAVIO TOOK THE check from me, handed me a folded piece of paper in exchange. "Eve was asking for 'Tiniest' a couple of days ago but I couldn't reach you on your cell. Your mom said she had to dictate the last scene of her memoir to you. So, you know, I wrote down what she said. If you want it."

I took the piece of paper from him, stashed it behind a lily vase on the fireplace mantle as he walked away.

"MAMA?" MAXITO PRESSED a straw into his blue juice box. "Where did all the crows go?"

"I don't know," I said. "They flew away."

Leslie and Leo ambled in now, two nights before the memorial, Leo carrying a plastic bag of my mother's remains.

"We couldn't afford an urn," Leslie said. "Do we have anything like an urn?"

I pulled a Mexican ceramic casserole dish from a low cupboard in the kitchen, offered it up.

Leo placed the bag inside. "Just right," he said.

The chef handed him a giant bag of corn husks and he washed them in the bathtub, took the scorpions he found outside.

We made masa, then made it again because the chef said the first batch wasn't good enough for a final send-off. And we all sat around the dining room table folding the masa and pork and cheese and chile into the clean corn husks.

Ana, the woman who organized the annual Day of the Dead procession to the old cemetery south of town texted: *May I play the accordion for your mother?*

I texted back: *Of course.*

And on the morning of the memorial, the lilacs along the gravel driveway up and decided to bloom.

Maia dug through family pictures and wedding announcements, cobbled together a photographic display of my mother's life.

I tore cilantro, cut limes.

The chef mixed the cabbage salad, made the green rice and calabacitas, steamed tamales.

Leslie built a fire in the backyard and someone put the *Harold and Maude* soundtrack on the boom box as the guests began to arrive – the caregivers and the nurses, Ronald and Sol, the strange blonde friend from the hospital and Moe Hawk, the worker my mother had fired for crying in the bathroom and Abra's friends from the Native Arts College. All the queers turned out, too, and my Buddhist friend from Albuquerque. There were people we didn't know, old friends we remembered from my stepdad's church community back in California, people who lived in New Mexico now.

Leslie scanned the crowd. "Where did they all come from?"

Cat Stevens on the boom box. I shrugged. "They're her friends. My friends."

Leslie shook her head. "Geez. If a cray cray dying lady can create community, maybe anybody can."

We borrowed chairs from the church across the street.

ABRA READ FROM The Bible. She read the Mary Oliver poem "Wild Geese."

An old man with a French accent who I recognized from the disconnected images of my childhood told a rambling story about taking my mother to all the sex shows in San Francisco in the '70s – Carol Doda and the rest of them – and the way his heart beat fast and nervous when he had to bring my mother home to her husband, the priest, and the way the priest didn't blink, just wanted to hear all about Carol Doda and the rest of them.

The chef set out the food, the tamales and the mole, the salad and the tortillas. She poured the wine.

I REMEMBERED OCTAVIO'S dictation notes. The piece of paper I'd stashed on the fireplace mantle. I unfolded it.

The final scene of my mother's memoir/screenplay had no dialogue.

> Eve walks slowly through the brush behind the house, walks toward and into the foothills. As she walks, the snow gets deeper, the visibility less. A mountain lion walks with her. Suddenly, a shot is heard from the direction of the house and there's a splattering of bright red blood on the white snow. The wind begins to hum. The snow falls more thickly. In the growing darkness and snow light, the ghost of a mountain lion walks up the mountain, and beside him the ghost of a woman.
>
> FADE TO BLACK.

LESLIE LIT THE fire in the backyard, handed out little slips of paper and instructed all the disparate guests to write down the thing they were ready to let go of. As Ana played the accordion, the people approached the fire and, one by one, they let something go.

36.
Ink and Story

MAXITO HELD MY HAND AS WE SHOPPED FOR BERRIES and braising greens at the farmer's market. He'd taken to wearing his Spider-Man costume everywhere we went, reveling in the winks and whispered attention: "Look, there goes a superhero!"

"We should buy peaches for Maia," he said, blinking into the early summer sun. "Maia likes beautiful things and peaches are beautiful."

Maia. She was scheduled to fly into Albuquerque with her new boyfriend that afternoon. She'd totaled Gammie's big red Oldsmobile in a weird morning accident on her last day of school and I'd offered to help her buy another used car with my ghostwriting paycheck.

Maxito hummed as he selected the peaches, each for its particular beauty. He tapped his Spider-Man foot to the drum beat of the one-man band who always played the farmer's market. "Nonna died," he announced to the poet he must have remembered from the candleshop when she appeared next to us at the peach table. She wore real rattlesnake rattlers as earrings.

"I heard about that," the poet said. "It must have been very sad." She looked at me. "Did you bury her here in the desert?"

"No," I said, then hesitated. "She's still on the mantle. Her ashes."

The poet picked up a peach. "Your mother wasn't from here. I don't think you should keep her here."

I didn't know why, but I knew the poet was right.

Maxito stared at her. "I'm not really Spider-Man," he said. "I'm just a kid. I'm Maxito."

The poet smiled at that. "Good to know."

AT HOME IN the former duplex, my painting of the winged house hung above the mantle now, my hobo birds in the dining room. I rushed inside, Maxito heavy on my hip, grabbed the ceramic casserole dish/urn with my free arm. I buckled Maxito back into his booster seat, seat-belted the urn into the front passenger seat and we all headed for the "pack and ship" on the south side of town.

MAXITO PLAYED WITH the toy UPS trucks and DHL planes as I pushed the casserole dish/urn across the counter.

The woman who worked there squinted. She had feathers for earrings. "Any declared value? What is it?"

"It's, um." I lifted the lid, set it down on the counter. "It's my mother." I'd jotted my godmother's address in Monterey on a note card, handed it to the woman.

She stood quiet for a moment, then back to business: "Well," she said. "We'll have to send your mother U.S. Postal Service. Certified. It's the only legal way." She hesitated. "May I?" And she motioned to lift the bag out of the urn.

It seemed an odd request, but I said, "Sure."

So she picked up that plastic bag full of ashes and bone fragments, said "it's surprisingly heavy."

I'd noticed that, too. The weight of it. "It's not nothing," I offered. "This living and dying thing."

The woman with feathers for earrings set the bag back in the urn, replaced the lid, and then she boxed up my mother for her freight-journey home to California.

"That's not Nonna," Maxito clarified, not bothering to look up from his toy trucks and planes. "It's just the ashes left over."

MY PHONE BUZZED with a text from the chef: *Do you want some alone time with your kids or should we make a big Southern dinner?*

I texted back: *Big Southern.*

IN THE CUSTOM kitchen, the chef mixed frying batter for the chicken and tofu cutlets, chopped bread for panzanella, said, "let's invite Carter Quark, too. He's family."

I boiled collards, stirred the cheese sauce for macaroni, chopped peaches for pie.

Pretty soon Maia and the new boyfriend appeared wearing black T-shirts and faded jeans; carrying bags of fresh mint and bottles of Old Crow Reserve. "We thought what's a big Southern dinner," the boyfriend said, "without juleps?"

Maia looked around, the art from her childhood on the walls, Maxito's robot drawings taped to the faux finishing in the kitchen, new red paper lanterns over my mother's old beige light fixtures. "It's cozy in here," she said. "Feels like home."

I grabbed her arm. "Let's see the new tattoo, Maia." I'd glimpsed it on Facebook. A living crow for her Nonna – just up her arm from the image of Gammie as a 1940s pin-up. Maia's matrilineage inked into her skin.

"I don't have any tattoos," Maxito chimed in. "But I do have a really cool shirt." And he pointed to the dinosaur on his belly. "It glows in the dark."

Maia showed off her arm piece, sighed. "It turned out pretty big."

"No, it's perfect," I said. "Beautiful."

All this ink and story. I thought about cold bricks at my back, thought about the wind in the alley just then for no reason. About the way abuse invents us, sure, but as long as we're alive there's time for reinvention; time to imagine some way to integrate the enormity of it all.

MY PHONE BUZZED with a text from Abra: *Landing in Barrow, Alaska.*

She'd headed to the Arctic to find the father and grandfather she'd never met. If life was finite, she figured, she might as well spend some time with this family of strangers at the edge of the earth. "That's what Baba Yaga would have me do, isn't it?" She'd asked over black coffee after my mother died.

And I'd nodded, "yes, I think so."

CARTER QUARK STEPPED in, set a six-pack of Dos Equis on the counter. "How does it feel now that it's all over?" he asked.

The urge was there, of course – to put a on bow on things, to say *we did this spiritual work and now we're enlightened.*

I didn't feel particularly enlightened.

I clicked my iPod into the music player – Mumford & Sons and Aloe Blacc and Nina Simone the rest of them.

Not enlightened, but it was true that something had lifted. Something had been burned through. The secrets and complicated violence we'd always called love – called home – were ashes now.

"Let's eat outside," I said.

Carter Quark set the picnic table with red napkins and my Gammie's silver.

The chef carried platters of fried chicken, collard greens and coleslaw.

"It's like Christmas," Maia's new boyfriend smiled.

But Carter shook his head. "This is just Tuesday here. They usually have a piñata."

"Don't worry," I promised. "We have a piñata."

Maxito wiggled into his seat at table. "With sugar in it."

MAIA HAD POSTED pictures of the chef frying tofu and the boyfriend mixing juleps on Facebook, so now Sol appeared in the backyard, too, a bottle of sparkling water in hand. "Mind if I join you?"

Maxito smiled up at her. "Come on."

Maia stood to give Sol a quick hug, but she pointed to me. "You have to ask Lady Yaga. She's the matriarch now."

I shrugged. *Why not?*

The chef leaned over my shoulder, whispered, "don't worry, she'll be nice."

"This all looks amazing," Maia said. She picked up a plate of biscuits, took one and passed it.

Maxito adjusted his Spider-Man mask. "I like biscuits," he sighed. "But I like sugar better."

I looked out over the backyard. A single crow on the fence.

I was once somebody's daughter.

And now I was free.

Notes and Acknowledgements

MANY PEOPLE'S NAMES AND A FEW PEOPLE'S IDENTIFYing characteristics have been changed to protect their privacy. Thanks to everyone else – not least of all Eve – for being good sports. My mother always wanted to be the star of something dark and grand. This probably isn't quite what she had in mind, but it's what I've got.

Thanks to all the wayward writers in the Literary Kitchen, where I teach and write – especially to my early draft editors Sailor Holladay, Krystee Sidwell, Deena Chafetz, Marti Reggio, Bonnie Ditlevsen, and the indomitable Inga Muscio.

And thanks to Rhonda Hughes and the no-nonsense team at Hawthorne Books for believing in it all. I'm thinking that right now some beautiful girl is sitting on the bank of a river with a copy of this book in her hands and right now she has a rose in her hair.